mexican
COOKING

Publications International, Ltd.
Favorite Brand Name Recipes at www.fbnr.com

All recipes and photographs that contain specific brand names are copyrighted by those companies and/or associations, unless otherwise specified. All photographs *except* those on pages 19, 29 and 69 copyright © Publications International, Ltd.

DOLE® is a registered trademark of Dole Food Company, Inc.

Some of the products listed in this publication may be in limited distribution.

Pictured on the front cover: Tamale Pie *(page 56).*
Pictured on the back cover *(top to bottom):* Southwestern Beef Stew *(page 45),* Zesty Steak Fajitas *(page 52)* and Mexican Slaw *(page 104).*

Illustrated by Anne Crosse.

ISBN-13: 978-1-4127-9581-4
ISBN-10: 1-4127-9581-8

Library of Congress Control Number: 2008923037

Manufactured in China.

8 7 6 5 4 3 2 1

Microwave Cooking: Microwave ovens vary in wattage. Use the cooking times as guidelines and check for doneness before adding more time.

Preparation/Cooking Times: Preparation times are based on the approximate amount of time required to assemble the recipe before cooking, baking, chilling or serving. These times include preparation steps such as measuring, chopping and mixing. The fact that some preparations and cooking can be done simultaneously is taken into account. Preparation of optional ingredients and serving suggestions is not included.

Contents

First Impressions

TORTILLA PIZZETTES

Makes about 30 pizzettes

1 cup chunky salsa
1 cup refried beans
2 tablespoons chopped fresh cilantro
½ teaspoon ground cumin
3 (10-inch) flour tortillas
1 cup (4 ounces) shredded Mexican cheese blend

1. Pour salsa into strainer; let drain at least 20 minutes.

2. Meanwhile, combine refried beans, cilantro and cumin in small bowl; mix well. Preheat oven to 400°F. Spray baking sheet lightly with nonstick cooking spray; set aside.

3. Cut each tortilla into 2½-inch circles with round cookie cutter (9 to 10 circles per tortilla). Spread each tortilla circle with refried bean mixture, leaving ¼ inch edge. Top each with a heaping teaspoonful drained salsa; sprinkle with about 1½ teaspoons cheese.

4. Place pizzettes on prepared baking sheet. Bake 7 minutes or until tortillas are golden brown.

Tortilla Pizzettes

Classic Guacamole

Makes about 2 cups

4 tablespoons finely chopped white onion, divided
1 or 2 serrano or jalapeño peppers,* seeded and finely chopped
1 tablespoon plus 1½ teaspoons chopped fresh cilantro, divided
¼ teaspoon chopped garlic
2 large ripe avocados
1 medium tomato, peeled and chopped
1 to 2 teaspoons lime juice
¼ teaspoon salt
Corn tortilla chips

*Serrano and jalapeño peppers can sting and irritate the skin; wear rubber gloves when handling peppers and do not touch eyes. Wash hands after handling.

1. Combine 2 tablespoons onion, serrano pepper, 1 tablespoon cilantro and garlic in large mortar. Grind with pestle until almost smooth. (Mixture can be processed in blender, if desired. It may become more watery than desired.)

2. Cut avocados lengthwise into halves; remove and discard pits. Scoop out avocado flesh; place in bowl. Add pepper mixture. Mash roughly, leaving avocado slightly chunky.

3. Add tomato, lime juice, salt, remaining 2 tablespoons onion and 1½ teaspoons cilantro to avocado mixture; mix well. Serve immediately or cover and refrigerate up to 4 hours. Serve with tortilla chips.

Classic Guacamole

CALIFORNIA QUESADILLAS

Makes 8 appetizer servings

1 small ripe avocado
2 packages (3 ounces each) cream cheese, softened
3 tablespoons *Frank's® RedHot®* Original Cayenne Pepper Sauce
¼ cup minced fresh cilantro leaves
16 (6-inch) flour tortillas (2 packages)
1 cup (4 ounces) shredded Cheddar or Monterey Jack cheese
½ cup finely chopped green onions
Sour cream (optional)

Halve avocado and remove pit. Scoop out flesh into food processor or bowl of electric mixer. Add cream cheese and ***Frank's RedHot*** Sauce. Cover and process or beat until smooth. Add cilantro; process or beat until well blended. Spread rounded tablespoon avocado mixture onto each tortilla. Sprinkle half the tortillas with cheese and onions, dividing evenly. Top with remaining tortillas; press gently.

Place tortillas on oiled grid. Grill over medium coals 5 minutes or until cheese melts and tortillas are lightly browned, turning once. Cut into triangles. Serve with sour cream, if desired. Garnish as desired.

Note: You may serve avocado mixture as a dip with tortilla chips.

Prep Time: 20 minutes
Cook Time: 5 minutes

California Quesadillas

Nachos à la Ortega®

Makes 4 to 6 servings

1 can (16 ounces) ORTEGA® Refried Beans, warmed
4 cups baked tortilla chips
1½ cups (6 ounces) shredded Monterey Jack cheese
2 tablespoons ORTEGA Jalapeños, sliced

SUGGESTED TOPPINGS

ORTEGA Salsa-Thick & Chunky, sour cream, guacamole, sliced ripe olives, chopped green onions, chopped fresh cilantro (optional)

PREHEAT broiler.

SPREAD beans over bottom of large ovenproof platter or 15×10-inch jelly-roll pan. Arrange chips over beans. Top with cheese and jalapeños.

BROIL for 1 to 1½ minutes or until cheese is melted. Top with desired toppings.

SOUTHWESTERN CHILE CHEESE EMPANADAS

Makes 32 appetizers

¾ cup (3 ounces) finely shredded taco cheese blend*
⅓ cup diced green chiles, drained
1 package (15 ounces) refrigerated pie crusts
1 egg
1 tablespoon water
Chili powder

If taco cheese blend is unavailable, toss ¾ cup shredded Monterey Jack cheese with ½ teaspoon chili powder.

1. Combine cheese and chiles in small bowl.

2. Unfold 1 pie crust on floured surface. Roll into 13-inch circle. Cut dough into 16 rounds using 3-inch cookie cutter, rerolling scraps as necessary. Repeat with remaining crust to total 32 circles.

3. Spoon 1 teaspoon cheese mixture in center of each dough round. Fold round in half, pressing to seal edge.

4. Place empanadas on waxed paper-lined baking sheets; freeze, uncovered, 1 hour or until firm. Place in resealable freezer food storage bags. Freeze up to 2 months, if desired.

5. To complete recipe, preheat oven to 400°F. Place frozen empanadas on ungreased baking sheets. Beat egg and water in small bowl; brush on empanadas. Sprinkle with chili powder.

6. Bake 12 to 17 minutes or until golden brown. Remove to wire racks to cool.

Serving Suggestion: Serve empanadas with salsa and sour cream.

Make-Ahead Time: up to 2 months in freezer
Final Prep Time: 30 minutes

HEARTY NACHOS

Makes 8 servings

1 pound ground beef
1 envelope LIPTON® RECIPE SECRETS® Onion Soup Mix
1 can (19 ounces) black beans, rinsed and drained
1 cup prepared salsa
1 package (8½ ounces) plain tortilla chips
1 cup shredded Cheddar cheese (about 4 ounces)

1. In 12-inch nonstick skillet, brown ground beef over medium-high heat; drain. Stir in soup mix, black beans and salsa. Bring to a boil over high heat. Reduce heat to low and simmer 5 minutes or until heated through.

2. Arrange tortilla chips on serving platter. Spread beef mixture over chips; sprinkle with Cheddar cheese. Top, if desired, with sliced green onions, sliced pitted ripe olives, chopped tomato and chopped cilantro.

CHILE-CHEESE QUESADILLAS WITH SALSA CRUDA

Makes 4 servings

2 tablespoons part-skim ricotta cheese
6 (6-inch) corn tortillas
½ cup (2 ounces) shredded Monterey Jack cheese
2 tablespoons diced mild green chiles
Nonstick cooking spray
Salsa Cruda (recipe follows)

Spread 2 teaspoons ricotta cheese over 1 tortilla. Sprinkle with heaping tablespoonful Monterey Jack cheese and 2 teaspoons diced chiles. Top with another tortilla. Repeat to make 2 more quesadillas. Spray small nonstick skillet with cooking spray; heat over medium-high heat. Add 1 quesadilla; cook 2 minutes or until bottom is golden. Turn; cook 2 minutes. Repeat with remaining quesadillas. Cut into wedges; serve with Salsa Cruda.

Salsa Cruda: Combine 1 cup chopped tomato, 2 tablespoons minced onion, 2 tablespoons minced fresh cilantro, 2 tablespoons lime juice, ½ jalapeño pepper, seeded and minced, and 1 minced garlic clove in small bowl; mix well. Makes 4 servings.

Hearty Nachos

FESTIVE TACO CUPS

Makes 36 taco cups

1 tablespoon vegetable oil
½ cup chopped onion
½ pound ground turkey or ground beef
1 clove garlic, minced
½ teaspoon dried oregano
½ teaspoon chili powder or taco seasoning
¼ teaspoon salt
1¼ cups (5 ounces) shredded taco cheese blend or Mexican cheese
   blend, divided
1 can (11½ ounces) refrigerated corn breadstick dough
Chopped fresh tomato and sliced green onion

1. Heat oil in large skillet over medium heat. Add onion; cook until tender. Add turkey; cook until turkey is no longer pink, stirring to break up meat. Stir in garlic, oregano, chili powder and salt. Remove from heat. Stir in ½ cup cheese; set aside.

2. Preheat oven to 375°F. Lightly grease 36 mini (1¾-inch) muffin cups. Remove dough from container but do not unroll dough. Separate dough into 8 pieces at perforations. Divide each piece into 3 pieces; roll or pat each piece into 3-inch circle. Press circles into prepared muffin cups.

3. Fill each cup with about 2 teaspoons turkey mixture. Bake 10 minutes. Sprinkle with remaining ¾ cup cheese; bake 2 to 3 minutes or until cheese is melted. Sprinkle with tomato and green onion.

Festive Taco Cups

GARDEN FRESH GAZPACHO

Makes 6 servings (6 cups)

4 large tomatoes (about 2 pounds)
1 large cucumber, peeled and seeded
½ red bell pepper, seeded
½ green bell pepper, seeded
½ red onion
3 cloves garlic
¼ cup *Frank's® RedHot®* Original Cayenne Pepper Sauce
¼ cup red wine vinegar
3 tablespoons olive oil
2 tablespoons minced fresh basil
1 teaspoon salt
Additional 2 cups chopped mixed fresh vegetables, such as
tomatoes, bell peppers, cucumbers and green onions

1. Coarsely chop 4 tomatoes, 1 cucumber, ½ red bell pepper, ½ green bell pepper, ½ red onion and garlic; place in food processor or blender. Add *Frank's RedHot* Sauce, vinegar, oil, basil and salt. Cover; process until very smooth. (Process in batches if necessary.) Transfer soup to large glass serving bowl.

2. Stir in additional chopped vegetables, leaving some for garnish, if desired. Cover; refrigerate 1 hour before serving.

Notas

Gazpacho is a spicy Spanish soup that is served cold. It is made of a puréed mixture of fresh tomatoes, green bell peppers, onions and cucumbers. It is most often flavored with garlic, olive oil and vinegar. This refreshing summer soup is often served garnished with croutons, chopped tomato, chopped green bell pepper and sliced green onion.

Garden Fresh Gazpacho

SPICY TUNA EMPANADAS

Makes 8 servings

1 (3-ounce) pouch of STARKIST Flavor Fresh Pouch® Albacore
   or Chunk Light Tuna
1 can (4 ounces) diced green chilies, drained
1 can (2¼ ounces) sliced ripe olives, drained
½ cup shredded sharp Cheddar cheese
1 chopped hard-cooked egg
   Salt and pepper to taste
¼ teaspoon hot pepper sauce
¼ cup medium thick and chunky salsa
2 packages (15 ounces each) refrigerated pie crusts
   Additional salsa

In medium bowl, place tuna, chilies, olives, cheese, egg, salt, pepper and
hot pepper sauce; toss lightly with fork. Add ¼ cup salsa and toss again;
set aside. Following directions on package, unfold pie crusts (roll out
slightly with rolling pin if you prefer thinner crust); cut 4 circles, 4 inches
each, out of each crust. Place 8 circles on foil-covered baking sheets; wet
edge of each circle with water. Top each circle with ¼ cup lightly packed
tuna mixture. Top with remaining circles, stretching pastry slightly to fit;
press edges together and crimp with fork. Cut slits in top crust to vent.
Bake in 425°F oven 15 to 18 minutes or until golden brown. Cool slightly.
Serve with additional salsa.

Spicy Tuna Empanadas

TURKEY HAM QUESADILLAS

Makes 8 servings

¼ cup picante sauce or salsa
 4 (7-inch) regular or whole wheat flour tortillas
½ cup (2 ounces) shredded Monterey Jack cheese
¼ cup finely chopped turkey ham or lean ham
¼ cup canned diced green chiles, drained *or* 1 to 2 tablespoons
    chopped jalapeño peppers*
Nonstick cooking spray
Additional picante sauce or salsa
Sour cream

*Jalapeño peppers can sting and irritate the skin; wear rubber gloves when handling peppers and do not touch eyes. Wash hands after handling.

1. Prepare grill for direct cooking.

2. Spread 1 tablespoon picante sauce on each tortilla.

3. Sprinkle cheese, turkey ham and chiles equally over half of each tortilla. Fold over to make quesadilla; spray both sides of quesadillas with cooking spray.

4. Place quesadillas on grid over medium heat. Grill, uncovered, 3 minutes or until cheese is melted and tortillas are golden brown, turning once. Cut into wedges; serve with additional picante sauce and sour cream.

Notas

Quesadillas are a versatile party food.
They can be made up to a day ahead and
refrigerated; reheat them on a baking sheet
in a preheated 375°F oven for 15 minutes.

Turkey Ham Quesadillas

BANDITO BUFFALO WINGS

Makes 6 servings

1 package (1.25 ounces) ORTEGA® Taco Seasoning Mix
12 (about 1 pound *total*) chicken wings
ORTEGA Salsa (any flavor)

PREHEAT oven to 375°F. Lightly grease 13×9-inch baking pan.

PLACE seasoning mix in heavy-duty plastic or paper bag. Add 3 chicken wings; shake well to coat. Place wings in prepared pan. Repeat until all wings have been coated.

BAKE for 35 to 40 minutes or until no longer pink near bone. Serve with salsa for dipping.

BITE SIZE TACOS

Makes 8 servings

1 pound ground beef
1 package (1.25 ounces) taco seasoning mix
2 cups *French's*® French Fried Onions, divided
¼ cup chopped fresh cilantro
32 bite-size round tortilla chips
¾ cup sour cream
1 cup shredded Cheddar cheese

1. Cook beef in nonstick skillet over medium-high heat 5 minutes or until browned; drain. Stir in taco seasoning mix, *¾ cup water, 1 cup* French Fried Onions and cilantro. Simmer 5 minutes or until flavors are blended, stirring often.

2. Preheat oven to 350°F. Arrange tortilla chips on foil-lined baking sheet. Top with beef mixture, sour cream, remaining *1 cup* onions and cheese.

3. Bake 5 minutes or until cheese is melted and onions are golden.

Prep Time: 5 minutes
Cook Time: 15 minutes

Bandito Buffalo Wings

CHILE CON QUESO

Makes 3 cups

2 tablespoons butter
¼ cup finely chopped onion
1 clove garlic, minced
1 can (8 ounces) tomato sauce
1 can (4 ounces) diced green chiles
2 cups (8 ounces) shredded Cheddar cheese
2 cups (8 ounces) shredded Monterey Jack cheese with
    jalapeño peppers
Tortilla chips and vegetable dippers

1. Melt butter in large saucepan over medium heat. Add onion and garlic; cook until onion is tender. Stir in tomato sauce and chiles; reduce heat to low. Simmer 3 minutes. Gradually add cheeses, stirring until cheeses are melted and mixture is evenly blended.

2. Transfer to fondue pot or chafing dish; keep warm over heat source. Serve with tortilla chips and vegetable dippers.

Chile con Queso

CHICKEN TORTILLA SOUP

Makes 4 servings

1 clove garlic, minced
1 can (14½ ounces) chicken broth
1 jar (16 ounces) mild chunky-style salsa
2 tablespoons *Frank's® RedHot®* Original Cayenne Pepper Sauce
1 package (10 ounces) fully cooked carved chicken breasts
1 can (8¾ ounces) whole kernel corn, undrained
1 tablespoon chopped fresh cilantro (optional)
1 cup crushed tortilla chips
½ cup (2 ounces) shredded Monterey Jack cheese

1. Heat *1 teaspoon oil* in large saucepan over medium-high heat. Cook garlic 1 minute or until tender. Add broth, *¾ cup water,* salsa and **Frank's RedHot** Sauce. Stir in chicken, corn and cilantro. Heat to boiling. Reduce heat to medium-low. Cook, covered, 5 minutes.

2. Stir in tortilla chips and cheese. Serve hot.

Prep Time: 5 minutes
Cook Time: 6 minutes

Chicken Tortilla Soup

NACHO CHEESE SOUP

Makes 6 servings

1 package (about 5 ounces) dry au gratin potatoes
1 can (about 15 ounces) whole kernel corn, undrained
2 cups water
1 cup salsa
2 cups milk
1½ cups (6 ounces) SARGENTO® Taco Blend Shredded Cheese
1 can (about 2 ounces) sliced ripe olives, drained
   Tortilla chips (optional)

In large saucepan, combine potatoes, dry au gratin sauce mix, corn with liquid, water and salsa. Heat to a boil; reduce heat. Cover and simmer 25 minutes or until potatoes are tender, stirring occasionally. Add milk, cheese and olives. Cook until cheese is melted and soup is heated through, stirring occasionally. Garnish with tortilla chips.

VEGETABLE CHILI

Makes 4 to 6 servings

2 cans (15 ounces each) chunky chili tomato sauce
1 bag (16 ounces) BIRDS EYE® frozen Farm Fresh Mixtures
   Broccoli, Corn and Red Peppers
1 can (15½ ounces) red kidney beans
1 can (4½ ounces) chopped green chilies
½ cup shredded Cheddar cheese

• Combine tomato sauce, vegetables, beans and chilies in large saucepan; bring to a boil.

• Cook, uncovered, over medium heat 5 minutes.

• Sprinkle individual servings with cheese.

Prep Time: 5 minutes
Cook Time: 10 minutes

Nacho Cheese Soup

ALBÓNDIGAS

Makes 6 servings

1 pound ground beef
½ small onion, finely chopped
¼ cup dry bread crumbs
1 egg
1 tablespoon chili powder
1 teaspoon ground cumin
½ teaspoon salt
3 cans (about 14 ounces each) chicken broth
1 medium carrot, thinly sliced
1 package (10 ounces) frozen corn or thawed frozen leaf spinach
¼ cup dry sherry

1. Mix beef, onion, bread crumbs, egg, chili powder, cumin and salt in medium bowl until well blended. Place mixture on lightly oiled cutting board; pat evenly into 1-inch-thick square. Cut into 36 squares with sharp knife; shape each square into a ball.

2. Place meatballs slightly apart in single layer in microwavable container. Cover; cook on HIGH 3 minutes or until meatballs are no longer pink in center.

3. Meanwhile, bring broth and carrot to a boil in covered Dutch oven over medium-high heat. Stir in corn and sherry. Transfer meatballs to broth with slotted spoon. Reduce heat to medium and simmer 3 to 4 minutes or until meatballs are cooked through. (Stir in spinach, if using, and simmer until heated through.)

Note: For a special touch, sprinkle soup with chopped fresh cilantro.

Prep and Cook Time: 30 minutes

BEEF FAJITA SOUP

Makes 8 servings

1 pound beef for stew
1 can (about 15 ounces) pinto beans, rinsed and drained
1 can (about 15 ounces) black beans, rinsed and drained
1 can (about 14 ounces) diced tomatoes with roasted garlic
1 can (about 14 ounces) beef broth
1 green bell pepper, thinly sliced
1 red bell pepper, thinly sliced
1 small onion, thinly sliced
1½ cups water
2 teaspoons ground cumin
1 teaspoon seasoned salt
1 teaspoon black pepper

SLOW COOKER DIRECTIONS

1. Combine beef, pinto beans, black beans, tomatoes, broth, bell peppers, onion, water, cumin, salt and black pepper in slow cooker.

2. Cover; cook on LOW 8 hours.

Serving Suggestion: Serve topped with sour cream, shredded Monterey Jack or Cheddar cheese and chopped olives.

Taco Soup

Makes 6 servings

1 pound BOB EVANS® Original Recipe or Zesty Hot Roll Sausage
1½ tablespoons olive oil
½ small Spanish onion, diced
1 jalapeño pepper, seeded and diced
1½ cups beef broth
1 cup peeled, seeded, diced fresh or canned tomatoes
1 cup vegetable juice
½ tablespoon ground cumin
½ tablespoon chili powder
¼ teaspoon salt
⅓ cup shredded Cheddar cheese
12 tortilla chips, broken into pieces

Crumble and cook sausage in olive oil in Dutch oven until no longer pink but not yet browned. Add onion and pepper; cook until onion is tender. Add remaining ingredients except cheese and chips; bring to a boil over high heat. Reduce heat to low and simmer, uncovered, 15 minutes. Ladle soup into bowls; garnish with cheese and chips. Refrigerate leftovers.

Taco Soup

SPICY PUMPKIN SOUP WITH GREEN CHILE SWIRL

Makes 4 servings

1 can (4 ounces) diced green chiles
¼ cup sour cream
¼ cup fresh cilantro leaves
1 can (15 ounces) solid-pack pumpkin
1 can (about 14 ounces) chicken broth
½ cup water
1 teaspoon ground cumin
½ teaspoon chili powder
¼ teaspoon garlic powder
⅛ teaspoon ground red pepper (optional)
Additional sour cream

1. Combine chiles, ¼ cup sour cream and cilantro in food processor or blender; process until smooth.

2. Combine pumpkin, broth, water, cumin, chili powder, garlic powder and red pepper, if desired, in medium saucepan; stir in ¼ cup green chile mixture. Bring to a boil over high heat; reduce heat to medium. Simmer, uncovered, 5 minutes, stirring occasionally.

3. Pour into serving bowls. Top each serving with small dollops of remaining green chile mixture and additional sour cream. Run tip of spoon through dollops to swirl.

Notas

*For extra flavor and crunch, sprinkle soup with
pepitas. Pepitas are dried pumpkin seeds that
have been roasted and salted. They are also a
tasty snack on their own.*

MEXICALI CHICKEN STEW

Makes 4 servings

1 package (1¼ ounces) taco seasoning, divided
12 ounces boneless skinless chicken thighs
   Nonstick cooking spray
2 cans (about 14 ounces each) stewed tomatoes with onions,
   celery and green peppers
1 package (10 ounces) frozen corn
1 package (9 ounces) frozen green beans
4 cups tortilla chips

1. Place half of taco seasoning in small bowl. Cut chicken thighs into 1-inch pieces. Add to bowl; toss to coat.

2. Coat large nonstick skillet with cooking spray. Cook and stir chicken 5 minutes over medium heat. Add tomatoes, corn, beans and remaining taco seasoning; bring to a boil. Reduce heat to medium-low; simmer 10 minutes. Top with tortilla chips before serving.

Serving Suggestion: Serve nachos with the stew. Spread tortilla chips on a plate; dot with salsa and sprinkle with cheese. Heat just until the cheese is melted.

Cook's Note: To lighten up this dish, simply substitute boneless skinless chicken breasts for the thighs.

Prep and Cook Time: 20 minutes

POZOLE

Makes 6 servings

1 tablespoon olive oil
1 large onion, thinly sliced
2 teaspoons dried oregano
1 clove garlic, minced
½ teaspoon ground cumin
2 cans (about 14 ounces each) chicken broth
1 package (10 ounces) frozen corn
1 to 2 cans (4 ounces each) chopped green chiles
1 can (2¼ ounces) sliced black olives, drained
¾ pound boneless skinless chicken breasts
Chopped fresh cilantro

1. Heat oil in Dutch oven over medium heat. Add onion, oregano, garlic and cumin. Cover and cook 6 minutes or until onion is tender, stirring occasionally.

2. Add broth, corn, chiles and olives. Cover and bring to a boil over high heat.

3. Meanwhile, cut chicken into thin strips. Add to soup. Reduce heat to medium-low; cover and cook 3 to 4 minutes or until chicken is cooked through. Sprinkle with cilantro.

Cook's Note: A Dutch oven is a heavy pot or kettle with a tight-fitting lid that prevents steam from escaping while cooking.

Prep and Cook Time: 20 minutes

Pozole

SOUTH-OF-THE-BORDER CORN AND ONION SOUP

Makes 6 to 8 servings

2 cans (13¾ ounces each) chicken broth
1 package (16 ounces) frozen whole kernel corn
1 cup mild taco sauce
1⅓ cups *French's*® French Fried Onions, divided
1 tablespoon *Frank's*® *RedHot*® Original Cayenne Pepper Sauce
½ teaspoon ground cumin
1 cup (4 ounces) shredded Cheddar or Monterey Jack cheese
    with jalapeño pepper
1 can (4 ounces) chopped green chilies, drained
1 cup low-fat sour cream

Combine chicken broth, corn, taco sauce, ⅔ *cup* French Fried Onions, *Frank's RedHot* Sauce and cumin in large saucepan. Bring to a boil over high heat, stirring often. Reduce heat to low. Simmer, uncovered, 10 minutes, stirring occasionally.

Pour one third of the soup into blender or food processor. Cover tightly; blend until puréed. Transfer to large bowl. Repeat with remaining soup, blending in batches. Return all puréed mixture to saucepan.

Add cheese; whisk until cheese melts and mixture is well blended. Stir in green chilies and sour cream. Cook over low heat until heated through. Do not boil. Ladle soup into individual bowls. Garnish with additional sour cream, if desired. Sprinkle with remaining ⅔ *cup* onions.

Prep Time: 30 minutes
Cook Time: 15 minutes

South-of-the-Border Corn and Onion Soup

TORTILLA SOUP

Makes 6 servings

1 tablespoon butter or margarine
½ cup chopped green bell pepper
½ cup chopped onion
½ teaspoon ground cumin
3½ cups (two 14½ ounce cans) chicken broth
1 jar (16 ounces) ORTEGA® Salsa-Thick & Chunky
1 cup whole-kernel corn
1 tablespoon vegetable oil
6 corn tortillas, cut into ½-inch strips
¾ cup (3 ounces) shredded 4 cheese Mexican blend
  Sour cream (optional)

MELT butter in medium saucepan over medium heat. Add bell pepper, onion and cumin; cook for 3 to 4 minutes or until tender. Stir in broth, salsa and corn. Bring to a boil. Reduce heat to low; cook for 5 minutes.

HEAT vegetable oil in medium skillet over medium-high heat. Add tortilla strips; cook for 3 to 4 minutes or until tender.

SERVE in soup bowls. Top with tortilla strips, cheese and a dollop of sour cream.

Notas

A tortilla is a round, thin unleavened baked Mexican bread. It can be made of either corn or wheat flour, water and a little salt. Traditionally the dough is shaped, flattened by hand and cooked on both sides on a hot griddle until dry and flecked with brown. Tortillas are a staple of Mexican and Tex-Mex cooking.

SOPA DE LIMA

Makes 6 servings

2 tablespoons extra-virgin olive oil
2 pounds chicken thighs and legs
1 cup chopped yellow onions
2 cloves garlic, minced
6 cups water
1 cup chopped seeded tomatoes
1 jalapeño pepper, minced* *or* ¼ teaspoon dried red pepper flakes
1 tablespoon chili powder
1 teaspoon ground cumin
1 teaspoon dried oregano
3 tablespoons lime juice
2 teaspoons salt
½ cup chopped cilantro leaves
¼ cup finely chopped radishes
    Lime wedges (optional)

*Jalapeño peppers can sting and irritate the skin; wear rubber gloves when handling peppers and do not touch eyes. Wash hands after handling.

1. Heat oil in Dutch oven over medium-high heat. Add chicken; cook on both sides until browned, about 4 minutes total. Remove to plate.

2. Add onion and garlic to Dutch oven. Reduce heat to medium; cook 3 to 4 minutes or until onions are translucent. Add water; bring to a boil over high heat. Add reserved chicken, tomatoes, jalapeño pepper, chili powder, cumin and oregano. Return to a boil. Reduce heat, cover and simmer 1 hour or until chicken is falling off the bone.

3. Remove chicken with slotted spoon; cool. Remove meat from bone, shred and return to Dutch oven with lime juice and salt.

4. Combine cilantro and radishes in small bowl. Garnish soup with radish mixture and lime wedges.

TACO BEAN CHILI

Makes 6 to 8 servings

½ cup dried kidney beans
½ cup dried pinto beans
½ cup dried red beans
4 cups water
1 pound ground beef or ground turkey, browned and drained
1 can (about 14 ounces) diced tomatoes with green chiles
1 can (8 ounces) tomato sauce
1 package (1¼ ounces) taco seasoning mix
1 tablespoon dried minced onion
½ teaspoon chili powder *or* chipotle chile powder
¼ teaspoon ground cumin
1½ cups tortilla chips

1. Place beans in large bowl; cover with water. Soak 6 to 8 hours or overnight. (To quick soak beans, place beans in large saucepan; cover with water. Bring to a boil over high heat. Boil 2 minutes. Remove from heat; let soak, covered, 1 hour.) Drain beans; discard water.

2. Place soaked beans, 4 cups water, ground beef, tomatoes, tomato sauce, seasoning mix, onion, chili powder and cumin in Dutch oven. Bring to a boil over high heat. Cover; reduce heat and simmer 1½ to 2 hours or until beans are tender.

3. Crush tortilla chips. Stir into chili and cook 5 to 10 minutes to thicken.

Taco Bean Chili

CHUNKY VEGETABLE CHILI

Makes 8 servings

2 tablespoons vegetable oil
1 medium onion, chopped
2 stalks celery, diced
1 carrot, diced
3 cloves garlic, minced
2 cans (about 15 ounces each) Great Northern beans,
    rinsed and drained
1½ cups water
1 cup frozen corn
1 can (6 ounces) tomato paste
1 can (4 ounces) diced mild green chiles, undrained
1 tablespoon chili powder
2 teaspoons dried oregano
1 teaspoon salt
Chopped fresh cilantro

1. Heat oil in large skillet over medium-high heat. Add onion, celery, carrot and garlic; cook 5 minutes or until vegetables are tender, stirring occasionally.

2. Stir beans, water, corn, tomato paste, chiles, chili powder, oregano and salt into skillet. Reduce heat to medium-low. Simmer 20 minutes, stirring occasionally. Sprinkle with cilantro.

SOUTHWESTERN BEEF STEW

Makes about 6 servings

1 tablespoon plus 1 teaspoon BERTOLLI® Olive Oil, divided
1½ pounds boneless beef chuck, cut into 1-inch cubes
1 can (4 ounces) chopped green chilies, drained
2 large cloves garlic, finely chopped
1 teaspoon ground cumin (optional)
1 can (14 to 16 ounces) whole or plum tomatoes, undrained and
    chopped
1 envelope LIPTON® RECIPE SECRETS® Onion or Beefy Onion
    Soup Mix
1 cup water
1 package (10 ounces) frozen cut okra or green beans, thawed
1 large red or green bell pepper, cut into 1-inch pieces
4 frozen half-ears corn-on-the-cob, thawed and each cut into 3 round
    pieces
2 tablespoons chopped fresh cilantro (optional)

In 5-quart Dutch oven or heavy saucepot, heat 1 tablespoon oil over medium-high heat and brown ½ of the beef; remove and set aside. Repeat with remaining beef; remove and set aside. In same Dutch oven, heat remaining 1 teaspoon oil over medium heat and cook chilies, garlic and cumin, stirring constantly, 3 minutes. Return beef to Dutch oven. Stir in tomatoes and onion soup mix blended with water. Bring to a boil over high heat. Reduce heat to low and simmer covered, stirring occasionally, 1 hour. Stir in okra, red pepper and corn. Bring to a boil over high heat. Reduce heat to low and simmer covered, stirring occasionally, 30 minutes or until meat is tender. Sprinkle with cilantro.

MEXICAN HOT POT

Makes 6 servings

1 tablespoon canola oil
1 onion, sliced
3 cloves garlic, minced
2 teaspoons red pepper flakes
2 teaspoons dried oregano
1 teaspoon ground cumin
1 can (28 ounces) diced tomatoes
2 cups corn
1 can (about 15 ounces) chickpeas, rinsed and drained
1 can (about 15 ounces) pinto beans, rinsed and drained
1 cup water
6 cups shredded iceberg lettuce

1. Heat oil in stockpot or Dutch oven over medium-high heat. Add onion and garlic; cook and stir 5 minutes. Add red pepper flakes, oregano and cumin; mix well.

2. Stir in tomatoes, corn, chickpeas, pinto beans and water; bring to a boil over high heat.

3. Reduce heat to medium-low; cover and simmer 15 minutes. Top individual servings with 1 cup shredded lettuce. Serve hot.

Notas

Chili powders, ground red pepper and red pepper flakes are all made from dried chiles. Whether you're working with fresh, dried or ground chiles, it is important to know that the longer you cook chiles, the hotter the dish will be. That's why a long simmered stew with chiles may be quite hot, while a quick stir-fry with chiles has more flavor and less heat.

Mexican Hot Pot

SOUTHWESTERN TWO BEAN CHILI & RICE

Makes 4 servings

1 bag (about ½ cup uncooked) boil-in-bag white rice
1 tablespoon vegetable oil
1 cup chopped onion
1 cup chopped green bell pepper
1½ teaspoons minced garlic
1 can (about 15 ounces) chili beans in sauce
1 can (about 15 ounces) black or pinto beans, rinsed and drained
1 can (10 ounces) diced tomatoes with green chiles
1 tablespoon chili powder
2 teaspoons ground cumin
1 cup (4 ounces) shredded Cheddar or Monterey Jack cheese

1. Cook rice according to package directions.

2. Meanwhile, heat oil in large saucepan over medium-high heat. Add onion, bell pepper and garlic; cook 5 minutes, stirring occasionally. Stir in chili beans, black beans, tomatoes, chili powder and cumin. Cover; bring to a boil over high heat. Reduce heat to medium-low. Simmer, covered, 10 minutes.

3. Transfer rice to 4 shallow bowls. Ladle bean mixture over rice; top with cheese.

Prep and Cook Time: 20 minutes

Southwestern Two Bean Chili & Rice

Bountiful Beef

CRUNCHY LAYERED BEEF & BEAN SALAD

Makes 6 servings

1 pound ground beef or turkey
2 cans (about 15 ounces each) black beans or pinto beans,
  rinsed and drained
1 can (about 14 ounces) stewed tomatoes, undrained
1⅓ cups *French's®* French Fried Onions, divided
1 tablespoon *Frank's® RedHot®* Original Cayenne Pepper Sauce
1 package (1¼ ounces) taco seasoning mix
6 cups shredded lettuce
1 cup (4 ounces) shredded Cheddar or Monterey Jack cheese

1. Cook beef in large nonstick skillet over medium heat until thoroughly browned; drain well. Stir in beans, tomatoes, ⅔ *cup* French Fried Onions, *Frank's RedHot* Sauce and taco seasoning. Heat to boiling. Cook over medium heat 5 minutes, stirring occasionally.

2. Spoon beef mixture over lettuce on serving platter. Top with cheese.

3. Microwave remaining ⅔ *cup* onions 1 minute on HIGH. Sprinkle over salad.

Prep Time: 10 minutes
Cook Time: 6 minutes

Crunchy Layered Beef & Bean Salad

ZESTY STEAK FAJITAS

Makes 4 servings

¾ cup *French's®* Worcestershire Sauce, divided
1 pound boneless top round, sirloin or flank steak
3 tablespoons taco seasoning mix
2 red or green bell peppers, cut into quarters
1 to 2 large onions, cut into thick slices
¾ cup chili sauce
8 (8-inch) flour or corn tortillas, heated
  Sour cream and shredded cheese (optional)

1. Pour ½ cup Worcestershire over steak in deep dish. Cover and refrigerate 30 minutes or up to 3 hours. Drain meat and rub both sides with seasoning mix.

2. Grill meat and vegetables over medium-hot coals 10 to 15 minutes until meat is medium rare and vegetables are charred, but tender.

3. Thinly slice meat and vegetables. Place in large bowl. Add chili sauce and ¼ cup Worcestershire. Toss to coat. Serve in tortillas and garnish with sour cream and cheese.

Prep Time: 5 minutes
Cook Time: 15 minutes
Marinate Time: 30 minutes

Zesty Steak Fajitas

FIESTA BEEF ENCHILADAS

Makes 6 servings

½ **pound ground beef**
½ **cup sliced green onions**
2 **teaspoons minced garlic**
1 **cup cooked white or brown rice**
1½ **cups chopped tomato, divided**
¾ **cup frozen corn, thawed**
1 **cup (4 ounces) shredded Mexican cheese blend or Cheddar cheese, divided**
½ **cup salsa or picante sauce**
12 **(6- to 7-inch) corn tortillas**
1 **can (10 ounces) mild or hot enchilada sauce**
1 **cup shredded romaine lettuce**

1. Preheat oven to 375°F. Spray 13×9-inch baking dish with nonstick cooking spray; set aside.

2. Brown beef in medium nonstick skillet over medium heat, stirring to break up meat; drain. Add green onions and garlic; cook and stir 2 minutes.

3. Add rice, 1 cup tomato, corn, ½ cup cheese and salsa to meat mixture; mix well. Spoon mixture down center of tortillas. Roll up; place seam side down in prepared dish. Spoon enchilada sauce evenly over enchiladas.

4. Cover with foil; bake 20 minutes or until heated through. Sprinkle with remaining ½ cup cheese; bake 5 minutes or until cheese melts. Top with lettuce and remaining ½ cup tomato.

Prep Time: 15 minutes
Cook Time: 35 minutes

Fiesta Beef Enchiladas

TAMALE PIE

Makes 6 servings

1 pound ground beef
1 tablespoon chili powder
2 cloves garlic
½ teaspoon salt
1 cup shredded Monterey Jack cheese
1 package (8½ ounces) corn muffin mix, plus ingredients
    to prepare mix
1 can (11 ounces) Mexican-style corn, drained
6 sheets (12×12 inches) heavy-duty foil, lightly sprayed with
    nonstick cooking spray
12 tablespoons salsa
6 tablespoons sour cream
6 cilantro sprigs

1. Preheat oven to 450°F.

2. Place beef, chili powder, garlic and salt in large skillet. Cook over medium-high heat 6 to 8 minutes or until meat is no longer pink, stirring to break up meat. Drain fat. Remove from heat; stir in cheese. Set aside.

3. Prepare corn muffin mix according to package directions. Stir in corn.

4. Place about ½ cup beef mixture in center of one foil sheet; flatten slightly. Top with ¼ cup corn bread batter. Spread lightly over beef. (It is not necessary to cover sides of beef.) Double fold sides and ends of foil to seal packet, leaving head space for heat circulation. Repeat with remaining beef and corn bread mixture to make 5 more packets. Place packets on baking sheet.

5. Bake 12 minutes. Let stand 5 minutes. Carefully open packets. Transfer contents to serving plates. Spoon 2 tablespoons salsa and 1 tablespoon sour cream over each pie. Top with cilantro.

TACO POT PIE

Makes 4 to 6 servings

1 pound ground beef
1 package (1¼ ounces) taco seasoning mix
¼ cup water
1 can (8 ounces) kidney beans, rinsed and drained
1 cup chopped tomato
¾ cup frozen corn, thawed
¾ cup frozen peas, thawed
1½ cups (6 ounces) shredded Cheddar cheese
1 can (11½ ounces) refrigerated corn breadstick dough

1. Preheat oven to 400°F. Brown beef in medium ovenproof skillet over medium-high heat, stirring to break up meat; drain. Add seasoning mix and water to skillet. Cook over medium-low heat 3 minutes or until most of liquid is absorbed, stirring occasionally.

2. Stir in beans, tomato, corn and peas. Cook 3 minutes or until mixture is heated through. Remove from heat; stir in cheese.

3. Separate corn breadstick dough into 16 strips. Twist strips, cutting to fit skillet. Arrange attractively over meat mixture. Press ends of dough lightly to edge of skillet to secure. Bake 15 minutes or until corn bread is golden brown and beef mixture is bubbly.

Prep and Cook Time: 30 minutes

CHIPOTLE TACO FILLING

Makes 8 cups filling

2 pounds ground beef
2 cans (about 15 ounces each) pinto beans, rinsed and drained
2 cups chopped yellow onions
1 can (about 14 ounces) diced tomatoes with peppers and onions, drained
4 chipotle peppers in adobo sauce, mashed
1 tablespoon sugar
1 tablespoon beef bouillon granules
1½ teaspoons ground cumin
   Taco shells or flour tortillas

SLOW COOKER DIRECTIONS

1. Brown beef in large nonstick skillet over medium-high heat, stirring to break up meat; drain.

2. Combine beef, beans, onions, tomatoes, peppers, sugar, bouillon and cumin in slow cooker. Cover; cook on LOW 4 hours or on HIGH 2 hours.

3. Serve in taco shells. Add shredded lettuce, salsa, shredded cheese and sour cream, if desired.

Notas

Chipotles are smoked, dried red jalapeño peppers. They have a rich, smoky, very hot flavor. They are commonly canned in adobo sauce, a flavorful blend of ground chiles, herbs and vinegar.

Chipotle Taco Filling

BEEF & SALSA SALAD SUPREME

Makes 4 servings

1 boneless beef top sirloin steak (about 1 pound)
2 teaspoons Mexican seasoning blend or chili powder
1 package (8 ounces) assorted torn salad greens or mesclun
  salad mix
1 cup drained rinsed canned black beans
1 cup frozen corn, thawed
¼ cup picante sauce or salsa
¼ cup red wine vinegar and oil salad dressing
1 medium tomato, seeded and chopped

1. Heat large nonstick skillet over medium heat. Rub both sides of steak with seasoning. Cook steak in skillet 5 minutes per side to medium-rare or until desired doneness. Transfer steak to carving board; tent with foil. Let stand 5 minutes.

2. Meanwhile, combine salad greens, beans and corn in large bowl. Combine picante sauce and dressing; add to greens mixture. Toss lightly to coat. Arrange on salad plates.

3. Carve steak crosswise into ¼-inch strips; arrange over salad greens, dividing evenly. Sprinkle with chopped tomato.

Serving Suggestion: For a special touch, add a sprig of fresh cilantro to each serving.

Prep and Cook Time: 20 minutes

Beef & Salsa Salad Supreme

STUFFED MEXICAN PIZZA PIE

Makes 6 servings

  1 pound ground beef
  1 large onion, chopped
  1 large green bell pepper, chopped
1½ cups UNCLE BEN'S® Instant Rice
  2 cans (14½ ounces each) Mexican-style stewed tomatoes, undrained
⅔ cup water
  2 cups (8 ounces) shredded Mexican-style seasoned Monterey Jack-
     Colby cheese blend, divided
  1 container (10 ounces) refrigerated pizza crust dough

1. Preheat oven to 425°F. Spray 13×9-inch baking pan with cooking spray; set aside.

2. Spray large nonstick skillet with nonstick cooking spray; heat over high heat until hot. Add beef, onion and bell pepper; cook and stir 5 minutes or until meat is no longer pink.

3. Add rice, stewed tomatoes and water. Bring to a boil. Pour beef mixture into prepared baking pan. Sprinkle with 1¼ cups cheese and stir until blended.

4. Unroll pizza crust dough on work surface. Place dough in one even layer over mixture in baking pan. Cut 6 to 8 slits in dough with sharp knife. Bake 10 minutes or until crust is lightly browned. Sprinkle top of crust with remaining ¾ cup cheese; continue baking 4 minutes or until cheese is melted and crust is deep golden brown.

5. Let stand 5 minutes before cutting.

Stuffed Mexican Pizza Pie

Easy Family Burritos

Makes 8 servings

1 boneless beef chuck roast (2 to 3 pounds)
1 jar (24 ounces) *or* 2 jars (16 ounces each) salsa
Flour tortillas

Slow Cooker Directions

1. Place roast in slow cooker; top with salsa. Cover; cook on LOW 8 to 10 hours.

2. Remove meat from slow cooker. Shred with 2 forks. Return to slow cooker; cook additional 1 to 2 hours.

3. Serve shredded meat wrapped in warm tortillas.

Notas

Burritos, originating in Mexico, are flour tortillas filled and folded into rectangular-shaped packages. Fillings vary and may include combinations of refried beans, shredded meat, poultry, chorizo, cheese, lettuce, tomatoes and sour cream. Breakfast burritos may be filled with seasoned scrambled eggs or a fruit mixture. Burritos are served without a sauce but may be garnished with sour cream or salsa.

Easy Family Burritos

CHILI-STUFFED POBLANO PEPPERS

Makes 4 servings

1 pound ground beef
4 large poblano peppers
1 can (about 15 ounces) chili beans in sauce
1 can (about 14 ounces) chili-style chunky tomatoes
1 tablespoon Mexican (adobo) seasoning
⅔ cup shredded Mexican cheese blend or Monterey Jack cheese

1. Preheat broiler. Fill large saucepan two-thirds full with water; bring to a boil over high heat. Brown beef in large nonstick skillet over medium-high heat 5 to 6 minutes, stirring to break up meat; drain.

2. Meanwhile, cut peppers in half lengthwise; remove stems and seeds. Add 4 pepper halves to boiling water; cook 3 minutes or until bright green and slightly softened. Remove; drain cut side down on plate. Repeat with remaining 4 halves. Set aside.

3. Add beans, tomatoes and Mexican seasoning to ground beef. Cook and stir over medium heat 5 minutes or until mixture thickens slightly.

4. Arrange peppers, cut side up, in 13×9-inch baking dish. Divide chili mixture evenly among each pepper; top with cheese. Broil 6 inches from heat 1 minute or until cheese is melted. Serve immediately.

Serving Suggestion: Serve with corn bread and chunky salsa.

Prep and Cook Time: 26 minutes

STEAK & PEPPER FAJITAS

Makes 4 servings

1 packet (1.12 ounces) fajita marinade
1 pound boneless steak,* cut into thin strips
1 bag (16 ounces) BIRDS EYE® frozen Farm Fresh
    Mixtures Pepper Stir Fry vegetables
8 (6- to 7-inch) flour tortillas, warmed
½ cup salsa

Or, substitute 1 pound boneless, skinless chicken, cut into strips.

• Prepare fajita marinade according to package directions.

• Add steak and vegetables. Let stand 10 minutes.

• Heat large skillet over medium-high heat. Remove steak and vegetables with slotted spoon and place in skillet.

• Add marinade, if desired. Cook 5 minutes or until steak is desired doneness and mixture is heated through, stirring occasionally.

• Wrap mixture in tortillas. Top with salsa.

Serving Suggestion: Serve with guacamole and sour cream, or serve mixture over rice instead of in flour tortillas.

Prep Time: 10 minutes
Cook Time: 5 to 7 minutes

TACO TWO-ZIES

Makes 10 tacos

1 pound ground beef
2 packages (1 ounce each) LAWRY'S® Taco Spices & Seasonings
⅔ cup water
1 can (1 pound 14 ounces) refried beans, warmed
10 small flour tortillas (fajita size), warmed to soften
10 jumbo size taco shells, heated according to package directions

TACO TOPPINGS
Shredded lettuce, shredded cheddar cheese and chopped tomatoes

In large skillet, brown ground beef over medium high heat until crumbly;
drain fat. Stir in 1 package Taco Spices & Seasonings and water. Bring
to a boil; reduce heat to low and cook, uncovered, 10 minutes, stirring
occasionally. In medium bowl, mix together beans and remaining package
Taco Spices & Seasonings. Spread about ⅓-cup seasoned beans all the way
to edges of each flour tortilla. Place a taco shell on center of each bean-
tortilla and fold edges up around shell, lightly pressing to 'stick' tortilla to
shell. Fill each taco with about 3 tablespoons taco meat. Top with your
choice of taco toppings.

Variations: May use lean ground turkey, chicken or pork in place of ground
beef. May use LAWRY'S® Chicken Taco Spices & Seasonings or LAWRY'S®
Hot Taco Spices & Seasonings instead of Taco Spices & Seasonings.

Prep Time: 8 to 10 minutes
Cook Time: 15 minutes

Taco Two-Zies

CHILI BEEF & RED PEPPER FAJITAS WITH CHIPOTLE SALSA

Makes 2 servings

6 ounces boneless beef top sirloin steak, thinly sliced
½ lime
1½ teaspoons chili powder
½ teaspoon ground cumin
½ cup diced plum tomatoes
¼ cup mild picante sauce
½ canned chipotle pepper in adobo sauce, mashed
Nonstick cooking spray
½ cup sliced onion
½ red bell pepper, cut into thin strips
2 (10-inch) flour tortillas, warmed
4 tablespoons sour cream
2 tablespoons chopped fresh cilantro

1. Place steak on plate. Squeeze lime juice over steak; sprinkle with chili powder and cumin. Let stand 10 minutes.

2. Meanwhile, to prepare salsa, combine tomatoes, picante sauce and chipotle in small bowl.

3. Coat 12-inch skillet with cooking spray; heat over high heat. Add onion and bell pepper; cook and stir 3 minutes or until edges begin to blacken. Remove from skillet. Lightly spray skillet with cooking spray away from heat. Add beef; cook and stir 1 minute. Return onion and bell pepper to skillet; cook 1 minute longer.

4. Place half of beef mixture in center of each tortilla; fold sides over filling. Top each tortilla with ¼ cup salsa, 2 tablespoons sour cream and 1 tablespoon cilantro.

Note: For a less spicy salsa, use less chipotle pepper or eliminate it completely.

Chili Beef & Red Pepper Fajitas with Chipotle Salsa

SHREDDED BEEF FAJITAS

Makes 12 servings

1 beef flank steak (about 1½ pounds)
1 cup chopped onion
1 green bell pepper, cut into ½-inch pieces
2 cloves garlic, minced *or* ¼ teaspoon garlic powder
1 package (about 1½ ounces) fajita seasoning mix
1 can (about 14 ounces) diced tomatoes with jalapeños
12 (8-inch) flour tortillas
Toppings: sour cream, guacamole, shredded Cheddar cheese, salsa

SLOW COOKER DIRECTIONS

1. Cut flank steak into 6 portions. Combine beef, onion, bell pepper, garlic and fajita seasoning mix. Add tomatoes. Cover; cook on LOW 8 to 10 hours or on HIGH 4 to 5 hours.

2. Remove beef from slow cooker; shred with 2 forks. Return beef to slow cooker and stir.

3. To serve fajitas, spoon beef mixture evenly onto flour tortillas. Add toppings as desired; roll up tortillas.

Shredded Beef Fajitas

Chicken Dinners

SALSA CHICKEN & RICE SKILLET

Makes 4 servings

1 (6.9-ounce) package RICE-A-RONI® Chicken Flavor
2 tablespoons margarine or butter
1 pound boneless, skinless chicken breasts, cut into 1-inch pieces
1 cup salsa
1 cup frozen or canned corn, drained
1 cup (4 ounces) shredded Cheddar cheese
1 medium tomato, chopped (optional)

1. In large skillet over medium heat, sauté rice-vermicelli mix with margarine until vermicelli is golden brown.

2. Slowly stir in 2 cups water, chicken, salsa and Special Seasonings. Bring to a boil. Reduce heat to low. Cover; simmer 15 minutes.

3. Stir in corn. Cover; simmer 5 minutes or until rice is tender and chicken is no longer pink inside. Top with cheese and tomato, if desired. Cover; let stand 5 minutes for cheese to melt.

Prep Time: 5 minutes
Cook Time: 30 minutes

Salsa Chicken & Rice Skillet

SOUTH-OF-THE-BORDER CUMIN CHICKEN

Makes 4 servings

1 package (16 ounces) frozen bell pepper stir-fry mixture *or* 3 bell peppers, thinly sliced*
4 chicken drumsticks
4 chicken thighs
1 can (about 14 ounces) stewed tomatoes
1 tablespoon mild pepper sauce
2 teaspoons sugar
1¾ teaspoons ground cumin, divided
1¼ teaspoons salt
1 teaspoon dried oregano
Hot cooked rice
1 to 2 medium limes, cut into wedges
¼ cup chopped fresh cilantro

If using fresh bell peppers, add 1 small onion, chopped.

SLOW COOKER DIRECTIONS

1. Place bell pepper mixture in slow cooker; place chicken on top.

2. Combine tomatoes, pepper sauce, sugar, 1 teaspoon cumin, salt and oregano in large bowl. Pour over chicken mixture. Cover; cook on LOW 8 hours or on HIGH 4 hours or until meat is just beginning to fall off bone.

3. Place chicken in shallow serving bowl. Stir remaining ¾ teaspoon cumin into tomato mixture and pour over chicken. Serve with rice and lime wedges. Sprinkle with cilantro.

South-of-the-Border Cumin Chicken

BARBECUED CHICKEN
WITH CHILE-ORANGE GLAZE

Makes 4 servings

1 to 2 dried de arbol chiles*
½ cup fresh orange juice
2 tablespoons tequila
2 cloves garlic, minced
1½ teaspoons grated orange peel
¼ teaspoon salt
¼ cup vegetable oil
1 broiler-fryer chicken (about 3 pounds), cut into quarters
Orange slices (optional)
Cilantro sprigs (optional)

For milder flavor, discard seeds from chiles. Since chiles can sting and irritate the skin, wear rubber gloves when handling peppers and do not touch eyes. Wash hands after handling chile peppers.

1. For marinade, crush chiles into coarse flakes in mortar with pestle. Combine chiles, orange juice, tequila, garlic, orange peel and salt in small bowl. Gradually add oil, whisking continuously, until thoroughly blended.

2. Arrange chicken in single layer in shallow glass baking dish. Pour marinade over chicken; turn pieces to coat. Marinate, covered, in refrigerator 2 to 3 hours, turning chicken several times.

3. Prepare grill for direct cooking or preheat broiler. Drain chicken, reserving marinade. Bring marinade to a boil in small saucepan over high heat; boil 2 minutes. Grill chicken on covered grill or broil 6 to 8 inches from heat 15 minutes, brushing frequently with marinade. Turn chicken. Grill or broil 15 minutes more or until chicken is cooked through and juices run clear, brushing frequently with marinade. *Do not baste during last 5 minutes of grilling.* Discard remaining marinade. Garnish with orange slices and cilantro.

Barbecued Chicken with Chile-Orange Glaze

CHICKEN AND BLACK BEAN SOFT TACOS

Makes 10 tacos

1 package (10) ORTEGA® Soft Taco Dinner Kit (flour tortillas, taco seasoning mix and taco sauce)
1 tablespoon vegetable oil
1 pound (3 to 4) boneless, skinless chicken breast halves, cut into 2-inch strips
1 medium onion, chopped
1 can (15 ounces) black beans, drained
¾ cup whole kernel corn
½ cup water
2 tablespoons lime juice

HEAT oil in large skillet over medium-high heat. Add chicken and onion; cook 4 to 5 minutes or until chicken is no longer pink in center. Stir in taco seasoning mix, beans, corn, water and lime juice. Bring to a boil. Reduce heat to low; cook, stirring occasionally, 5 to 6 minutes or until mixture is thickened.

REMOVE tortillas from outer plastic pouch. Microwave using HIGH (100%) power 10 to 15 seconds or until warm.

FILL each tortilla with ½ cup chicken mixture. Serve with taco sauce.

Chicken and Black Bean Soft Tacos

CHICKEN FAJITAS

Makes 4 servings

1 tablespoon vegetable oil
1 large green bell pepper, thinly sliced
1 large red bell pepper, thinly sliced
1 large onion, thinly sliced
1 clove garlic, minced
4 boneless skinless chicken breasts (about 1 pound), cut
    into ½-inch strips
½ teaspoon dried oregano
2 tablespoons dry white wine or water
    Salt and black pepper
8 (8-inch) flour tortillas
    Guacamole (optional)

1. Heat oil in large skillet over medium-high heat. Add bell peppers, onion and garlic. Cook 3 to 4 minutes or until crisp-tender, stirring occasionally. Remove vegetables with slotted spoon; set aside.

2. Add chicken and oregano to skillet. Cook 4 minutes or until chicken is cooked through, stirring occasionally.

3. Return vegetables to skillet. Add wine. Season with salt and black pepper. Cover and cook 2 minutes or until heated through.

4. Stack tortillas and wrap in foil. Heat tortillas in preheated 350°F oven 10 minutes or until warm. Fill tortillas with chicken mixture; serve with guacamole.

Chicken Fajitas

ARROZ CON POLLO

Makes 4 to 6 servings

4 slices bacon
1½ pounds (about 6) boneless, skinless chicken breasts
1 cup (1 small) chopped onion
1 cup (1 small) chopped green bell pepper
2 large cloves garlic, finely chopped
2 cups long-grain white rice
1 jar (16 ounces) ORTEGA® Salsa (any flavor)
1¾ cups (14½-ounce can) chicken broth
1 cup (8-ounce can) tomato sauce
1 teaspoon salt
½ teaspoon ground cumin
Chopped fresh parsley

COOK bacon in large saucepan over medium-high heat until crispy; remove from saucepan. Crumble bacon; set aside. Add chicken to saucepan; cook, turning frequently, for 5 to 7 minutes or until golden on both sides. Remove from saucepan; keep warm. Discard all but 2 tablespoons drippings from saucepan.

ADD onion, bell pepper and garlic; cook for 3 to 4 minutes or until crisp-tender. Add rice; cook for 2 to 3 minutes. Stir in salsa, chicken broth, tomato sauce, salt and cumin. Bring to a boil. Place chicken over rice mixture; reduce heat to low. Cover. Cook for 20 to 25 minutes or until most of moisture is absorbed and chicken is no longer pink in center. Sprinkle with bacon and parsley.

Arroz con Pollo

CILANTRO-LIME CHICKEN

Makes 4 servings

1 pound boneless skinless chicken breasts
2 small onions
1 large lime
2 tablespoons canola oil
1 or 2 small green or red jalapeño peppers,* seeded and sliced
1 small piece fresh ginger (1 inch long), peeled and thinly sliced
2 tablespoons chopped fresh cilantro
2 tablespoons soy sauce
1 to 2 teaspoons sugar
Hot cooked rice

Jalapeño peppers can sting and irritate the skin; wear rubber gloves when handling peppers and do not touch eyes. Wash hands after handling.

1. Cut each chicken breast into 8 pieces. Cut each onion into 8 wedges.

2. Remove 3 strips of peel from lime with vegetable peeler. Cut lime peel into very fine shreds. Juice lime; measure 2 tablespoons juice. Set aside.

3. Heat large skillet over medium-high heat 1 minute. Drizzle oil into skillet; heat 30 seconds. Add chicken, jalapeño pepper and ginger; cook and stir 3 minutes or until chicken is cooked through.

4. Reduce heat to medium. Add onions; cook and stir 5 minutes.

5. Add 2 teaspoons lime peel, lime juice and cilantro; cook and stir 1 minute. Add soy sauce and sugar; cook and stir until heated through. Serve with rice.

CHICKEN TOSTADAS

Makes 6 servings

  6 (8-inch) flour tortillas
    Nonstick cooking spray
  1 can (about 15 ounces) black beans, rinsed and drained
  ½ cup hot salsa
  2 teaspoons chili powder, divided
  1 teaspoon ground cumin, divided
 12 ounces chicken tenders
  2 cups finely chopped tomatoes, drained
  1 cup chopped onion
1½ cups (6 ounces) shredded Cheddar cheese
  2 cups shredded romaine or iceberg lettuce

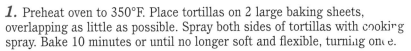

1. Preheat oven to 350°F. Place tortillas on 2 large baking sheets, overlapping as little as possible. Spray both sides of tortillas with cooking spray. Bake 10 minutes or until no longer soft and flexible, turning once.

2. Meanwhile, place beans in food processor and process until smooth. Transfer to medium saucepan. Stir in salsa, 1 teaspoon chili powder and ½ teaspoon cumin; simmer over medium heat 5 minutes or until heated through.

3. Cut chicken into ½-inch pieces. Sprinkle with remaining 1 teaspoon chili powder and ½ teaspoon cumin. Coat large nonstick skillet with cooking spray; heat over medium heat. Add chicken; cook and stir 5 minutes or until cooked through.

4. Spread bean mixture on tortillas to within ½ inch of edges. Top with chicken, tomatoes and onion. Sprinkle with cheese. Bake 2 minutes or just until cheese is melted. Top with lettuce; serve immediately.

Note: For a special touch, top each tostada with a dollop of sour cream.

Prep and Cook Time: 28 minutes

CHICKEN ENCHILADA SKILLET CASSEROLE

Makes 4 servings

1 bag (16 ounces) BIRDS EYE® frozen Farm Fresh Mixtures
    Broccoli, Corn & Red Peppers
3 cups shredded cooked chicken
1 can (16 ounces) diced tomatoes, undrained
1 package (1¼ ounces) taco seasoning mix
1 cup shredded Monterey Jack cheese
8 ounces tortilla chips

• In large skillet, combine vegetables, chicken, tomatoes and seasoning mix; bring to boil over medium-high heat.

• Cover; cook 4 minutes or until vegetables are cooked and mixture is heated through.

• Sprinkle with cheese; cover and cook 2 minutes more or until cheese is melted.

• Serve with chips.

Prep Time: 5 minutes
Cook Time: 10 minutes

Chicken Enchilada Skillet Casserole

BLACK BEAN GARNACHAS

Makes 4 servings

1 can (14½ ounces) DEL MONTE® Diced Tomatoes with Garlic
   & Onion
1 can (15 ounces) black or pinto beans, drained
2 cloves garlic, minced
1 to 2 teaspoons minced jalapeño peppers (optional)
½ teaspoon ground cumin
1 cup cubed grilled chicken
4 flour tortillas
½ cup (2 ounces) shredded sharp Cheddar cheese

1. Combine undrained tomatoes, beans, garlic, jalapeño peppers and cumin in large skillet. Cook over medium-high heat 5 to 7 minutes or until thickened, stirring occasionally. Stir in chicken. Season with salt and pepper, if desired.

2. Arrange tortillas in single layer on grill over medium coals. Spread about ¾ cup chicken mixture over each tortilla. Top with cheese.

3. Cook about 3 minutes or until bottoms of tortillas are browned and cheese is melted. Top with shredded lettuce, diced avocado and sliced jalapeño peppers, if desired.

Variation: Prepare chicken mixture as directed above. Place a tortilla in a dry skillet over medium heat. Spread with about ¾ cup chicken mixture; top with 2 tablespoons cheese. Cover and cook about 3 minutes or until bottom of tortilla is browned and cheese is melted. Repeat with remaining tortillas.

Prep Time: 5 minutes
Cook Time: 10 minutes

Black Bean Garnacha

SASSY CHICKEN & PEPPERS

Makes 2 servings

2 teaspoons Mexican seasoning*
2 boneless skinless chicken breasts
2 teaspoons canola oil
1 small red onion, sliced
½ medium red bell pepper, cut into thin strips
½ medium yellow or green bell pepper, cut into thin strips
¼ cup chunky salsa or chipotle salsa
1 tablespoon lime juice

If Mexican seasoning is not available, substitute 1 teaspoon chili powder, ½ teaspoon ground cumin, ½ teaspoon salt and ⅛ teaspoon ground red pepper.

1. Sprinkle seasoning over both sides of chicken; set aside.

2. Heat oil in large nonstick skillet over medium heat. Add onion; cook 3 minutes, stirring occasionally.

3. Add bell pepper strips; cook 3 minutes, stirring occasionally. Stir salsa and lime juice into vegetables.

4. Push vegetables to edges of skillet; add chicken to skillet. Cook 5 minutes; turn. Cook 4 minutes or until chicken is no longer pink in the center and vegetables are tender.

5. Transfer chicken to plates; top with vegetable mixture.

Sassy Chicken & Peppers

FAJITAS ON A STICK

Makes 8 fajitas

1 pound boneless, skinless chicken breasts, cut into 1-inch pieces
½ green bell pepper, cut into ½-inch pieces
½ onion, sliced into ½-inch slices
16 cherry tomatoes
8 wooden skewers, soaked in water for 30 minutes
1 cup LAWRY'S® Tequila Lime Marinade With Lime Juice
8 fajita size flour tortillas, warmed to soften

Thread chicken, pepper, onion and tomatoes onto skewers, dividing up ingredients equally. Brush heavily and frequently with Tequila Lime Marinade while grilling. Cook chicken 18 minutes or until thoroughly cooked. Place cooked skewer on warm tortilla; remove fajitas from skewer and roll-up tortilla to enclose fajita mixture securely. Serve immediately.

Variation: Also great using LAWRY'S® Mesquite Marinade With Lime Juice.

Prep Time: 20 minutes
Cook Time: 15 to 18 minutes

SAUSAGE STUFFED CHICKEN BREAST OLÉ

Makes 6 servings

6 boneless, skinless chicken breast halves
1 pound BOB EVANS® Original Recipe or Zesty Hot Roll Sausage
1 (8-ounce) block Monterey Jack cheese, divided
4 tablespoons butter or margarine, divided
1 large green bell pepper, sliced into rings
1 large onion, sliced into rings
2 cloves garlic, minced
2 (16-ounce) cans stewed tomatoes, undrained
1 (12-ounce) can large black olives, drained, sliced and divided
¼ cup chopped fresh cilantro
3 tablespoons chopped jalapeño peppers (optional)
   Sour cream (optional)
   Fresh cilantro sprigs (optional)

Pound chicken into uniform thin rectangles with meat mallet or rolling pin. Divide uncooked sausage into 6 equal pieces. Cut 6 (½-inch-thick) sticks from cheese block. Shred remaining cheese; set aside. Wrap each sausage piece around each cheese stick to enclose cheese completely. Place each sausage bundle on each chicken piece at one narrow end; roll up and secure with toothpicks. Melt 2 tablespoons butter in large Dutch oven or skillet over medium heat until hot. Add chicken bundles; cook, covered, about 5 to 7 minutes on each side or until browned, turning occasionally. Remove chicken; set aside.

Melt remaining 2 tablespoons butter in same Dutch oven. Add bell pepper, onion and garlic; cook and stir until lightly browned. Stir in tomatoes with juice, half the olives, chopped cilantro and jalapeños, if desired. Cook and stir over medium-low heat about 10 minutes. Add reserved chicken bundles. Cook, covered, 30 to 40 minutes or until flavors blend. To serve, spoon tomato sauce mixture on top of chicken. Sprinkle with remaining cheese and olives, if desired. Garnish with dollop of sour cream and cilantro sprigs, if desired. Serve hot. Refrigerate leftovers.

GREEN CHILE-CHICKEN CASSEROLE

Makes 6 servings

4 cups shredded cooked chicken

1½ cups green enchilada sauce

1 can (10¾ ounces) condensed cream of chicken soup, undiluted

1 container (8 ounces) sour cream

1 can (4 ounces) diced green chiles

½ cup vegetable oil

12 (6-inch) corn tortillas

1½ cups (6 ounces) shredded Colby-Jack cheese, divided

1. Preheat oven to 325°F. Grease 13×9-inch casserole.

2. Combine chicken, enchilada sauce, soup, sour cream and chiles in large skillet. Cook and stir over medium-high heat until warm.

3. Heat oil in separate deep skillet. Fry tortillas just until crisp; drain on paper towels. Place 4 tortillas on bottom of prepared casserole. Layer with ⅓ of chicken mixture and ½ cup cheese. Repeat layers twice.

4. Bake 15 to 20 minutes or until cheese is melted and casserole is heated through.

Tip: Shredded Mexican cheese blend can be substituted for Colby-Jack cheese.

Green Chile-Chicken Casserole

MEXICALI CHICKEN

Makes 4 servings

2 medium green bell peppers, cut into thin strips
1 large onion, quartered and thinly sliced
4 chicken thighs
4 chicken drumsticks
1 tablespoon chili powder
2 teaspoons dried oregano
1 jar (16 ounces) chipotle salsa
½ cup ketchup
2 teaspoons ground cumin
½ teaspoon salt
Hot cooked noodles

SLOW COOKER DIRECTIONS

1. Place bell peppers and onion in slow cooker; top with chicken. Sprinkle chili powder and oregano evenly over chicken; add salsa. Cover; cook on LOW 7 to 8 hours or on HIGH 2 to 3 hours.

2. Remove chicken pieces to serving bowl; keep warm. Stir ketchup, cumin and salt into liquid in slow cooker. Cook, uncovered, on HIGH 15 minutes or until heated through.

3. Pour mixture over chicken. Serve with noodles.

Tip: For thicker sauce, stir 2 tablespoons water into 1 tablespoon cornstarch until smooth. Stir into cooking liquid with ketchup, cumin and salt.

Prep Time: 10 minutes
Cook Time: 7 to 8 hours (LOW) • 2 to 3 hours (HIGH)

Mexicali Chicken

SOUTHWEST CHICKEN WITH CILANTRO SALSA

Makes 4 servings

4 boneless skinless chicken breasts
4 tablespoons lime juice, divided
  Black pepper
½ cup lightly packed fresh cilantro, chopped
⅓ cup thinly sliced or minced green onions
¼ to ½ jalapeño pepper,* seeded and minced
2 tablespoons pine nuts, toasted (optional)

Jalapeño peppers can sting and irritate the skin. Wear rubber gloves when handling peppers and do not touch eyes. Wash hands after handling.

1. Preheat broiler. Spray broiler pan with nonstick cooking spray.

2. Brush chicken with 2 tablespoons lime juice. Place on prepared pan. Sprinkle with black pepper. Broil chicken 2 inches from heat 8 to 10 minutes or until chicken is no longer pink in center.

3. Meanwhile, combine remaining 2 tablespoons lime juice, cilantro, onions, jalapeño pepper and pine nuts, if desired, in small bowl. Serve with chicken.

Notas

*Cilantro is a fresh leafy herb that looks
a lot like Italian parsley. Its distinctive flavor
complements spicy foods, especially Mexican,
Caribbean, Thai and Vietnamese dishes.*

Southwest Chicken with Cilantro Salsa

SPICY SPANISH RICE

Makes 4 servings

1 teaspoon canola oil
1 cup uncooked white rice
1 medium onion, chopped
2 cups chicken stock or canned low-sodium chicken broth, defatted
1 cup GUILTLESS GOURMET® Salsa (Roasted Red Pepper or
    Southwestern Grill)
  Green chili pepper strips (optional)

Heat large skillet over medium-high heat until hot. Add oil; swirl to coat
skillet. Add rice; cook and stir until lightly browned. Remove rice to small
bowl. Add onion to same skillet; cook and stir until onion is translucent. Add
stock and salsa to skillet; return rice to skillet. Bring to a boil. Reduce heat
to low; cover and simmer until liquid is absorbed and rice is tender. Serve
hot. Garnish with pepper, if desired.

Spicy Spanish Rice

MEXICAN SLAW

Makes 8 servings

1 corn tortilla, cut into thin strips
  Nonstick cooking spray
¼ teaspoon chili powder
3 cups shredded green cabbage
1 cup shredded red cabbage
½ cup shredded carrots
½ cup sliced radishes
½ cup corn
¼ cup coarsely chopped fresh cilantro
¼ cup mayonnaise
1 tablespoon lime juice
2 teaspoons vinegar
1 teaspoon honey
½ teaspoon cumin
¼ teaspoon salt
¼ teaspoon black pepper

1. Preheat oven to 350°F. Evenly arrange tortilla strips on nonstick baking sheet. Spray strips with cooking spray and sprinkle with chili powder. Bake 6 to 8 minutes or until strips are crisp. Remove from oven and set aside.

2. Place all remaining ingredients in large bowl; toss until well blended. Top with tortilla strips before serving.

Mexican Slaw

SOUTH-OF-THE-BORDER BAKED POTATO TOPPER

Makes 8 servings

1½ teaspoons butter
 1 cup broccoli florets
 1 clove garlic, minced
 ½ teaspoon ground cumin
 ½ cup (2 ounces) shredded Monterey Jack cheese
 ¼ cup mayonnaise
 ¼ cup sour cream
 ¼ teaspoon salt
 ⅛ teaspoon black pepper
 4 large hot baked potatoes, cut into halves
   Chili powder

1. Melt butter in medium saucepan over medium heat. Add broccoli, garlic and cumin. Cook and stir 3 to 4 minutes or until broccoli is crisp-tender. Remove from heat and cool slightly.

2. Add cheese, mayonnaise and sour cream to saucepan. Stir well to blend. Add salt and pepper. Spoon over hot baked potato halves. Sprinkle with chili powder.

Notas

*For quick and easy "baked" potatoes, pierce
the potato in several places with a fork and
place on a paper towel in the microwave. Heat
on HIGH 5 to 6 minutes. Let stand about 5
minutes. For crisper skin, wrap the potato in
a paper towel after cooking, but before stand
time. For soft skin, wrap the potato in foil after
cooking,
but before stand time.*

CALABACITAS

Makes 4 to 6 servings

2 tablespoons vegetable oil
2 medium yellow crookneck squash, cut into ¼-inch slices
2 medium zucchini, cut into ¼-inch slices
1 medium onion, coarsely chopped
1 clove garlic, minced
1 can (8 ounces) whole kernel corn, drained
¼ cup diced green chiles
½ teaspoon salt
¼ teaspoon dried oregano
⅛ teaspoon black pepper
½ cup (2 ounces) shredded mild Cheddar cheese

1. Heat oil in large skillet over medium heat. Add squash, zucchini, onion and garlic. Cook, stirring occasionally, until onion is tender. Reduce heat to medium-low. Cover and cook 10 minutes or until squash are barely tender.

2. Add corn, chiles, salt, oregano and pepper. Cook 3 minutes or until heated through.

3. Sprinkle with cheese; heat just until cheese melts.

GREEN RICE PILAF

Makes 4 to 6 servings

2 tablespoons vegetable oil
1 cup uncooked long-grain white rice (not converted)
¼ cup finely chopped white onion
2 poblano or Anaheim peppers,* roasted, peeled, seeded,
    deveined and chopped
6 green onions, sliced
1 clove garlic, minced
¼ teaspoon salt
¼ teaspoon ground cumin
1¾ cups chicken broth
1½ cups shredded queso Chihuahua or Monterey Jack cheese, divided
⅓ cup coarsely chopped fresh cilantro

Peppers can sting and irritate the skin; wear rubber gloves when handling peppers and do not touch eyes. Wash hands after handling.

1. Preheat oven to 375°F. Heat oil in large skillet over medium heat. Add rice; cook and stir 2 minutes or until rice turns opaque.

2. Add white onion; cook and stir 1 minute. Stir in peppers, green onions, garlic, salt and cumin; cook and stir 20 seconds.

3. Stir in broth. Bring to a boil over high heat. Reduce heat to low. Cover and simmer 15 minutes or until rice is almost tender.

4. Remove skillet from heat. Add 1 cup cheese and cilantro; toss lightly to mix. Transfer to greased 1½-quart baking dish; top with remaining ½ cup cheese.

5. Bake, uncovered, 15 minutes or until rice is tender and cheese topping is melted.

Green Rice Pilaf

CHILE RELLENOS CASSEROLE

Makes 8 servings

1½ cups (6 ounces) shredded Monterey Jack *or* cheddar cheese, divided
1 can (4 ounces) ORTEGA® Diced Green Chiles
2 tablespoons all-purpose flour
1½ cups milk
3 eggs, lightly beaten

GARNISH SUGGESTIONS

ORTEGA Salsa-Thick & Chunky, sour cream, sliced ripe olives, chopped green onions

PREHEAT oven to 325°F. Lightly grease 8-inch-square baking dish.

SPRINKLE ¾ cup cheese onto bottom of prepared baking dish. Top with chiles and remaining cheese. Place flour in medium bowl. Gradually add milk, stirring until smooth. Stir in eggs; pour mixture over cheese.

BAKE for 45 to 50 minutes or until knife inserted in center comes out clean. Let stand for 10 minutes.

SERVE with salsa and desired toppings.

SPICY SOUTHWESTERN VEGETABLE SAUTÉ

Makes 6 servings

1 bag (16 ounces) frozen green beans
2 tablespoons water
1 tablespoon olive oil
1 medium red bell pepper, chopped
1 medium yellow summer squash or zucchini, chopped
1 jalapeño pepper,* seeded and chopped (optional)
½ teaspoon ground cumin
½ teaspoon garlic powder
½ teaspoon chili powder
¼ cup sliced green onions
2 tablespoons chopped fresh cilantro
1 tablespoon brown sugar

Jalapeños can sting and irritate the skin; wear rubber gloves when handling peppers and do not touch eyes. Wash hands after handling.

1. Heat large skillet over medium heat; add green beans, water and oil. Cover; cook 4 minutes, stirring occasionally.

2. Add bell pepper, squash, jalapeño pepper, if desired, cumin, garlic powder and chili powder. Cook, uncovered, stirring occasionally, 4 minutes or until vegetables are crisp-tender. Stir in green onions, cilantro and brown sugar.

SALSA MACARONI & CHEESE

Makes 4 servings

1 jar (1 pound) RAGÚ® Cheese Creations!® Double Cheddar Sauce
1 cup prepared mild salsa
8 ounces elbow macaroni, cooked and drained

1. In 2-quart saucepan, heat Ragú Cheese Creations! Sauce over medium heat. Stir in salsa; heat through.

2. Toss with hot macaroni. Serve immediately.

Prep Time: 5 minutes
Cook Time: 15 minutes

Notas

*Each year Americans eat more than
2 billion pounds of pasta. That comes to
9 pounds for every person.*

Salsa Macaroni & Cheese

COLACHE

Makes 6 to 8 servings

2 tablespoons vegetable oil
1 butternut squash (about 2 pounds), peeled, seeded and diced
1 medium onion, coarsely chopped
1 clove garlic, minced
1 can (about 14 ounces) diced tomatoes
1 green bell pepper, cut into 1-inch pieces
1 can (14½ ounces) corn, drained
1 canned green chile, coarsely chopped (optional)
½ teaspoon salt
¼ teaspoon black pepper

1. Heat oil in large skillet over medium heat. Add squash, onion and garlic; cook 5 minutes or until onion is tender. Add tomatoes and bell pepper. Bring to a boil over high heat. Cover; reduce heat and simmer 15 minutes.

2. Add remaining ingredients. Simmer, covered, 5 minutes or until squash is tender. Uncover; increase heat to high. Continue cooking until most of liquid has evaporated.

Colache

RAJAS

Makes 4 servings

1 large red bell pepper, halved lengthwise
2 to 3 poblano peppers or green bell peppers
1 tablespoon olive oil
1 medium onion, cut in ¼-inch wedges
3 cloves garlic, minced
1 teaspoon dried oregano
½ teaspoon salt
1 cup (4 ounces) shredded Monterey Jack cheese
¼ cup chopped fresh cilantro

1. Preheat broiler and cover broiler pan with foil. Place bell and poblano peppers on pan; broil 12 minutes or until pepper skins are charred, turning poblano peppers several times. Remove peppers to medium bowl. Cover with plastic wrap; let stand 20 minutes. Remove charred skins, stems and seeds. Cut peppers into thin strips.

2. Heat oil in 12-inch nonstick skillet over medium-high heat. Add onion; cook and stir 5 minutes or until crisp-tender. Add garlic, oregano and salt; cook and stir 1 minute.

3. Transfer pepper mixture to casserole; top with cheese and cilantro. Broil until cheese is melted.

Rajas

Confetti Black Beans

Makes 6 servings

  1 cup dried black beans
  3 cups water
  1 can (about 14 ounces) chicken broth
  1 bay leaf
1½ teaspoons olive oil
  1 medium onion, chopped
 ¼ cup chopped red bell pepper
 ¼ cup chopped yellow bell pepper
  2 cloves garlic, minced
  1 jalapeño pepper,* finely chopped
  1 large tomato, seeded and chopped
 ½ teaspoon salt
 ⅛ teaspoon black pepper
   Hot pepper sauce

Jalapeño peppers can sting and irritate the skin; wear rubber gloves when handling peppers and do not touch eyes. Wash hands after handling.

1. Sort and rinse black beans. Cover with water and soak overnight; drain. Place beans in large saucepan with chicken broth; bring to a boil over high heat. Add bay leaf. Reduce heat to low; cover and simmer about 1½ hours or until beans are tender.

2. Heat oil in large skillet over medium heat. Add onion, bell peppers, garlic and jalapeño pepper; cook 8 to 10 minutes or until onion is tender, stirring frequently. Add tomato, salt and black pepper; cook 5 minutes.

3. Add onion mixture to beans; cook 15 to 20 minutes. Remove bay leaf before serving. Serve with hot pepper sauce.

Confetti Black Beans

MEXICAN-STYLE RICE AND CHEESE

Makes 6 to 8 servings

1 can (about 15 ounces) Mexican-style beans
1 can (about 14 ounces) diced tomatoes with jalapeños
2 cups (8 ounces) shredded Monterey Jack or Colby cheese, divided
1½ cups uncooked converted rice
1 large onion, finely chopped
½ (8-ounce) package cream cheese
3 cloves garlic, minced

SLOW COOKER DIRECTIONS

1. Grease inside of slow cooker. Combine beans, tomatoes, 1 cup cheese, rice, onion, cream cheese and garlic in slow cooker; mix well.

2. Cover; cook on LOW 6 to 8 hours.

3. Just before serving, sprinkle with remaining 1 cup cheese.

Notas

Converted, or parboiled rice, is the unhulled grain that is soaked, processed by steam pressure and dried before milling. This procedure gelatinizes the starch in the grain, and ensures a firmer, more separate grain. Parboiled rice is favored by consumers who desire separate rice grains and for use in the slow cooker.

Mexican-Style Rice and Cheese

GREEN CHILE RICE

Makes 6 servings

1 cup uncooked white rice
1 can (about 14 ounces) chicken broth plus water to measure 2 cups
1 can (4 ounces) chopped mild green chiles
½ medium yellow onion, peeled and diced
1 teaspoon dried oregano
½ teaspoon salt
½ teaspoon cumin seeds
3 green onions, thinly sliced
⅓ to ½ cup fresh cilantro leaves

1. Combine rice, broth, chiles, yellow onion, oregano, salt and cumin in large saucepan. Bring to a boil over high heat. Reduce heat to low; cover and simmer 18 minutes or until liquid is absorbed and rice is tender.

2. Stir in green onions and cilantro.

Green Chile Rice

Sweets and Drinks

SPANISH CHURROS

Makes about 3 dozen churros

 1 cup water
 6 tablespoons sugar, divided
 ¼ cup (½ stick) butter
 ¼ teaspoon salt
 1 cup all-purpose flour
 2 eggs
   Vegetable oil for frying
 1 teaspoon ground cinnamon

1. Place water, 2 tablespoons sugar, butter and salt in medium saucepan; bring to a boil over high heat. Remove from heat; add flour. Beat with spoon until dough forms ball and releases from side of pan. Vigorously beat in eggs, 1 at a time, until mixture is smooth. Spoon dough into pastry bag fitted with large star tip. Pipe 3×1-inch strips onto waxed paper-lined baking sheet. Freeze 20 minutes.

2. Pour vegetable oil into 10-inch skillet to ¾-inch depth. Heat oil to 375°F. Transfer frozen dough to hot oil with large spatula. Fry 4 or 5 churros at a time until deep golden brown, 3 to 4 minutes, turning once. Remove churros with slotted spoon to paper towels; drain.

3. Combine remaining 4 tablespoons sugar with cinnamon. Place in paper bag. Add warm churros, 1 at a time; close bag and shake until coated with sugar mixture. Remove to wire rack. Repeat with remaining sugar mixture and churros; cool completely. Store tightly covered at room temperature or freeze up to 3 months.

Spanish Churros

RICE PUDDING MEXICANA

Makes 6 servings

1 package (4-serving size) instant rice pudding
1 tablespoon vanilla
¼ teaspoon ground cinnamon
   Dash ground cloves
¼ cup slivered almonds
   Additional ground cinnamon

1. Prepare rice pudding according to package directions.

2. Remove pudding from heat; stir in vanilla, ¼ teaspoon cinnamon and cloves. Pour evenly into 6 individual dessert dishes.

3. Sprinkle evenly with almonds and additional cinnamon. Serve warm.

Prep and Cook Time: 18 minutes

PINEAPPLE MARGARITA

Makes 2 servings

⅔ cup DOLE® Pineapple Juice
1½ ounces tequila
1 ounce Triple Sec
   Juice of 1 lemon
   Crushed ice

• Combine pineapple juice, tequila, Triple Sec and lemon juice in blender. Add ice; blend until slushy. Serve in frosted glasses. *(Do not put salt on rim.)*

Rice Pudding Mexicana

FIRE AND ICE

Makes 6 servings

2 cups vanilla ice cream
2 teaspoons finely chopped jalapeño pepper*
1 teaspoon grated lime peel, divided
1 cup water
¼ cup sugar
1 cup peeled and chopped kiwi
1 tablespoon lime juice
1 cup fresh raspberries

Jalapeño peppers can sting and irritate the skin; wear rubber gloves when handling peppers and do not touch eyes. Wash hands after handling.

1. Soften ice cream slightly in small bowl. Stir in jalapeño pepper and ½ teaspoon lime peel. Freeze until firm.

2. Combine water, sugar and remaining ½ teaspoon lime peel in small saucepan; bring to a boil over high heat. Boil 5 minutes or until reduced by about one third. Remove from heat; cool to room temperature.

3. Place kiwi and lime juice in blender or food processor; process until smooth. Stir in water mixture. Pour through fine strainer to remove kiwi seeds and lime peel, pressing liquid through strainer with back of spoon. Refrigerate kiwi mixture until cold.

4. Pour ¼ cup kiwi mixture into each of 6 chilled bowls. Scoop ⅓ cup jalapeño ice cream in center of each bowl. Sprinkle raspberries evenly on top.

Fire and Ice

PUMPKIN FLAN

Makes 8 servings

1 can (16 ounces) solid-pack pumpkin
1 can (12 ounces) evaporated milk
1⅔ cup granulated sugar, divided
3 eggs, beaten
2 teaspoons vanilla, divided
1 teaspoon ground cinnamon
½ teaspoon ground ginger
½ teaspoon ground cloves
½ teaspoon ground nutmeg
¼ cup whipping cream
1 tablespoon powdered sugar

1. Preheat oven to 300°F. Beat pumpkin, evaporated milk, ⅓ cup granulated sugar, eggs, 1 teaspoon vanilla and spices in large bowl with electric mixer at medium speed until blended. Set aside.

2. Heat remaining 1⅓ cups granulated sugar in large saucepan over medium-high heat, stirring until melted and golden brown. *Mixture will be hot.* Carefully pour sugar into eight (4-ounce) ramekins. Place ramekins in 15×11-inch baking dish and fill each ramekin with pumpkin mixture.

3. Pour hot water into pan until filled half way up sides of ramekins. Bake 45 to 55 minutes or until knife inserted into centers comes out clean. Remove from oven; cool. Run knife around edges of each ramekin to loosen. Invert onto serving plates.

4. Beat whipping cream, powdered sugar and remaining 1 teaspoon vanilla in small bowl with electric mixer at high speed until soft peaks form. Garnish each flan with whipped cream mixture.

Cook's Note: The flan can also be baked in a 9-inch pie pan for 60 minutes.

MARGARITAS

Makes 4 servings

8 ounces tequila
4 ounces Triple Sec
8 ounces fresh lime juice
¼ cup sugar
    Crushed ice
    Additional lime juice (for glass rims, optional)
    Coarse or kosher salt (for glass rims, optional)

In blender jar, mix tequila, Triple Sec, lime juice, sugar and crushed ice until frothy. Dip rim of glass in lime juice, then in salt, if desired. Fill with margarita mixture.

Meal Idea: Serve in an iced pitcher with all your favorite Mexican entrees or appetizers. Great for parties.

Variations: May use about 8 ounces sweet-and-sour bar mix in place of fresh lime juice and sugar. To make Strawberry Margaritas, blend in about 1 to 1½ cups fresh strawberries.

Prep Time: 10 to 15 minutes

Favorite recipe from **Lawry's® Foods**

MEXICAN CHOCOLATE COOKIES

Makes 4 dozen cookies

1½ cups all-purpose flour
2 teaspoons ground cinnamon
1 teaspoon baking soda
½ teaspoon salt
2 cups (12 ounces) semisweet chocolate chips
¾ cup (1½ sticks) unsalted butter, softened
½ cup toasted whole almonds
½ cup packed brown sugar
¼ cup granulated sugar
2 eggs
1 teaspoon almond extract

1. Preheat oven to 375°F. Combine flour, cinnamon, baking soda and salt in medium bowl; set aside.

2. Melt chocolate chips and butter in medium saucepan over medium heat, stirring until smooth. Remove from heat; cool to room temperature.

3. Pulse almonds, brown sugar and granulated sugar in food processor until finely ground; transfer mixture to large bowl. Beat in chocolate mixture, eggs and almond extract. Gradually stir in flour mixture.

4. Drop by level tablespoonfuls onto ungreased baking sheets. Bake 8 to 9 minutes or until edges are set but centers are still slightly soft. Cool on baking sheets 2 to 3 minutes; remove to wire racks to cool.

PIÑA COLADA MILKSHAKE

Makes 4 servings

2 cups (1 pint) coconut sorbet
2 cups (1 pint) vanilla frozen yogurt or ice cream
¾ cup pineapple juice
¼ cup dark rum (optional)

Combine all ingredients in blender. Blend until smooth.

DULCE DE LECHE DESSERT SANDWICHES

Makes 6 servings

1 pint (2 cups) Dulce de Leche ice cream
¾ cup pecans
12 chocolate cookies

1. Preheat oven to 350°F.

2. Remove ice cream from freezer; let stand at room temperature 10 minutes or until slightly softened.

3. Place pecans in single layer in a shallow baking pan. Bake 8 minutes or until golden and fragrant; set aside to cool. Finely chop pecans; reserve.

4. Spread ⅓ cup ice cream onto flat sides of half the cookies. Place remaining cookies, flat sides down, on ice cream; press cookies together lightly. Use a spatula to smooth or remove excess ice cream, if necessary. Wrap each sandwich individually in plastic wrap; freeze 30 minutes or until firm.

5. Coat ice cream edges with pecans; rewrap in plastic. Freeze an additional 30 minutes.

Note: Ice cream sandwiches should be eaten within three days. After three days, cookies will absorb moisture and become soggy.

CHOCOLATE-RUM PARFAITS

Makes 4 servings

6 to 6½ ounces Mexican chocolate, coarsely chopped*
1½ cups whipping cream, divided
3 tablespoons golden rum (optional)
¾ teaspoon vanilla
  Whipped cream
  Sliced almonds
  Cookies

Or, substitute 6 ounces semisweet coarsely chopped chocolate, 1 tablespoon ground cinnamon and ¼ teaspoon almond extract.

1. Combine chocolate and 3 tablespoons cream in top of double boiler. Heat over simmering water until chocolate is melted and smooth, stirring occasionally. Gradually stir in rum, if desired; remove top pan from heat. Let stand at room temperature 15 minutes to cool slightly.

2. Combine remaining cream and vanilla in chilled deep bowl. Beat with electric mixer at low speed; gradually increase speed until stiff peaks form.

3. Gently fold whipped cream into cooled chocolate mixture until uniform in color. Spoon chocolate mixture into 4 individual dessert dishes. Refrigerate 2 to 3 hours until firm. Top with whipped cream and almonds. Serve with cookies.

Chocolate-Rum Parfaits

MEXICAN WEDDING COOKIES

Makes about 4 dozen cookies

1 cup pecan pieces or halves
1 cup (2 sticks) butter, softened
2 cups powdered sugar, divided
2 cups all-purpose flour, divided
2 teaspoons vanilla
⅛ teaspoon salt

1. Place pecans in food processor. Process using on/off pulsing action until pecans are finely ground but not pasty.

2. Beat butter and ½ cup powdered sugar in large bowl with electric mixer at medium speed until light and fluffy. Gradually add 1 cup flour, vanilla and salt. Beat at low speed until well blended. Stir in remaining 1 cup flour and pecans. Shape dough into ball; wrap in plastic wrap and refrigerate 1 hour or until firm.

3. Preheat oven to 350°F. Shape dough into 1-inch balls. Place 1 inch apart on ungreased cookie sheets.

4. Bake 12 to 15 minutes or until golden brown. Cool on cookie sheets 2 minutes.

5. Meanwhile, place 1 cup powdered sugar in 13×9-inch glass dish. Transfer warm cookies to powdered sugar. Roll cookies in powdered sugar, coating well. Let cookies cool in sugar.

6. Sift remaining ½ cup powdered sugar over sugar-coated cookies before serving. Store tightly covered at room temperature or freeze up to 1 month.

Mexican Wedding Cookies

LACY TORTILLA HEARTS

Makes 4 servings

4 (8-inch) flour tortillas
3 tablespoons butter or margarine, melted
2 tablespoons vegetable oil
Powdered sugar

1. Cut out ¾- to 1-inch heart shapes evenly throughout tortillas; discard hearts. Place tortillas in 15×10×1-inch jelly-roll pan.

2. Combine butter and oil in small bowl; brush evenly over tortillas. Let stand 15 minutes.

3. Preheat oven to 400°F.

4. Place tortillas in single layer in additional jelly-roll pans or on rimmed baking sheets. Bake 7 to 10 minutes or until crisp. Place tortillas on wire racks or waxed paper-lined baking sheets. Cool completely. Sprinkle generously with powdered sugar.

Variation: Omit powdered sugar. Combine 1 tablespoon red colored sugar with ⅛ teaspoon cinnamon; mix well. Sprinkle over warm tortillas.

MANGO-LIME COOLER

Makes 4 servings

2 cups cold water
2 large mangos, peeled, seeded and cubed
1 cup ice
½ cup sugar
½ cup freshly squeezed lime juice (about 6 limes)

Combine all ingredients in blender. Process on high speed until smooth.

Notas

*Although largely overlooked by most
Americans until recently, mangos are one of
the most popular fruits in the world. This lushly
aromatic and flavorful fruit is used abundantly
in Indian, Mexican and Caribbean cuisines.
Native to Southeast Asia, mangos have been
cultivated for more than 6,000 years. Now,
there are hundreds of varieties, ranging in
weight from less than half a pound to four
pounds or more. When properly ripe, mangoes
have a floral aroma, succulent orange flesh and
tropical fruity taste.*

CARAMEL FLAN

Makes 6 to 8 servings

1 cup sugar, divided
2 cups half-and-half
1 cup milk
1½ teaspoons vanilla
6 eggs
2 egg yolks
Hot water as needed

1. Preheat oven to 325°F. Heat 5½- to 6-cup ring mold in oven 10 minutes or until hot.

2. Heat ½ cup sugar in medium heavy skillet over medium-high heat 5 to 8 minutes or until sugar is completely melted and deep amber color, stirring frequently. *Do not allow sugar to burn.*

3. Immediately pour caramelized sugar into ring mold. Holding mold with potholder, quickly rotate to coat bottom and sides evenly with sugar. Place mold on wire rack. *Caution: Caramelized sugar is very hot; do not touch it.*

4. Combine half-and-half and milk in medium heavy saucepan. Heat over medium heat until almost simmering; remove from heat. Add remaining ½ cup sugar and vanilla; stir until sugar is dissolved.

5. Lightly beat eggs and egg yolks in large bowl until blended but not foamy; gradually stir in milk mixture. Pour custard into ring mold.

6. Place mold in large baking pan; pour hot water into baking pan to depth of ½ inch. Bake 35 to 40 minutes or until knife inserted into center of custard comes out clean.

7. Remove mold from water bath; place on wire rack. Let stand 30 minutes. Cover and refrigerate 1½ to 2 hours or until thoroughly chilled.

8. To serve, loosen inner and outer edges of flan with tip of small knife. Cover mold with rimmed serving plate; invert and lift off mold. Spoon melted caramel over each serving.

Caramel Flan

Toasted Almond Horchata

Makes 8 to 10 servings

3½ cups water, divided
2 (3-inch) cinnamon sticks
1 cup uncooked instant white rice
1 cup slivered almonds, toasted
3 cups cold water
¾ to 1 cup sugar
½ teaspoon vanilla
Lime slices

1. Combine 3 cups water and cinnamon sticks in medium saucepan. Cover and bring to a boil over high heat. Reduce heat to medium-low. Simmer 15 minutes. Remove from heat; let cool to temperature of hot tap water. Measure cinnamon water to equal 3 cups, adding additional hot water if needed.

2. Place rice in food processor; process using on/off pulsing action 1 to 2 minutes or until rice is powdery. Add almonds; process until finely ground (mixture will begin to stick together). Remove rice mixture to medium bowl; stir in cinnamon water and cinnamon sticks. Let stand 1 hour or until mixture is thick and rice grains are soft.

3. Remove cinnamon sticks; discard. Pour mixture into food processor. Add remaining ½ cup water; process 2 to 4 minutes or until mixture is very creamy. Strain mixture through fine-meshed sieve or several layers of dampened cheesecloth into half-gallon pitcher. Stir in 3 cups cold water, sugar and vanilla; stir until sugar is completely dissolved.

4. Garnish with lime slices.

Toasted Almond Horchata

CAJETA Y FRUTAS

Makes 12 servings

1 (14-ounce) can sweetened condensed milk
3 cups whipped topping
Sliced strawberries, peaches or grapes and mint

1. Simmer milk in double boiler 1 to 2 hours until milk is light caramel colored, stirring occasionally.

2. Pour cooked milk into mixer bowl with paddle attachment. Beat with electric mixer at low speed until milk is smooth and creamy. Bring milk to room temperature. Fold in whipped topping; stir just until smooth. Transfer to bowl; cover and refrigerate 2 hours or overnight.

3. Serve in small dishes; garnish with fruit and mint.

Cajeta y Frutas

MEXICAN SUGAR COOKIES (POLVORONES)

Makes about 2 dozen cookies

1 cup (2 sticks) butter, softened
½ cup powdered sugar
2 tablespoons milk
1 teaspoon vanilla
1 teaspoon ground cinnamon, divided
1½ to 1¾ cups all-purpose flour
1 teaspoon baking powder
1 cup granulated sugar plus additional as needed
1 square (1 ounce) semisweet chocolate, finely grated

1. Preheat oven to 325°F. Grease cookie sheets; set aside.

2. Beat butter, powdered sugar, milk, vanilla and ½ teaspoon cinnamon in large bowl with electric mixer at medium speed until light and fluffy, scraping down side of bowl once. Gradually add 1½ cups flour and baking powder. Beat at low speed until well blended, scraping down side of bowl once. Stir in additional flour with spoon if dough is too soft to shape.

3. Shape tablespoonfuls of dough into 1¼-inch balls. Place balls 3 inches apart on prepared cookie sheets. Flatten each ball into 2-inch round with bottom of glass dipped in granulated sugar.

4. Bake 20 to 25 minutes or until edges are golden brown. Let stand on cookie sheets 3 to 4 minutes.

5. Meanwhile, combine 1 cup granulated sugar, chocolate and remaining ½ teaspoon cinnamon in small bowl. Transfer cookies, one at a time, to sugar mixture; coat both sides. Remove to wire racks; cool completely.

6. Store tightly covered at room temperature or freeze up to 3 months.

Mexican Sugar Cookies (Polvorones)

NEW MEXICAN HOT CHOCOLATE

Makes 4 servings

¼ cup sugar
¼ cup unsweetened cocoa powder
½ teaspoon ground cinnamon
¼ teaspoon ground nutmeg
Dash salt
⅔ cup water
3⅓ cups milk
1 teaspoon vanilla
4 cinnamon sticks or dash ground nutmeg

1. Combine sugar, cocoa, ground cinnamon, ¼ teaspoon nutmeg, salt and water in large saucepan. Cook, stirring occasionally, over medium heat until cocoa and sugar are dissolved. Add milk and vanilla; bring to a simmer.

2. Whisk until frothy. Pour into 4 mugs. Place one cinnamon stick in each mug.

BISCOCHITOS

Makes 4 to 5 dozen cookies

3 cups all-purpose flour
2 teaspoons anise seeds
1½ teaspoons baking powder
½ teaspoon salt
1 cup (2 sticks) butter
¾ cup sugar, divided
1 egg
¼ cup orange juice
2 teaspoons ground cinnamon

1. Preheat oven to 350°F. Combine flour, anise seeds, baking powder and salt in medium bowl; set aside. Beat butter in large bowl with electric mixer at medium speed until creamy. Add ½ cup sugar; beat until fluffy. Blend in egg. Gradually add flour mixture alternately with orange juice, mixing well after each addition.

continued on page 150

Top to bottom: New Mexican Hot Chocolate and Biscochitos

Biscochitos, continued

2. Divide dough in half. Roll out one half on lightly floured surface to ¼-inch thickness; cover remaining dough to prevent drying. Cut dough with 2- to 2½-inch cookie cutters; gather scraps and re-roll. If dough becomes too soft to handle, refrigerate briefly. Place cookies 1 inch apart on ungreased cookie sheets.

3. Combine remaining ¼ cup sugar and cinnamon; lightly sprinkle over cookies. Bake 8 to 10 minutes or until edges are lightly browned. Remove to wire racks; cool completely. Store in airtight container.

HONEY SOPAIPILLAS

Makes 16 sopaipillas

¼ **cup plus 2 teaspoons sugar, divided**
½ **teaspoon ground cinnamon**
 2 **cups all-purpose flour**
 2 **teaspoons baking powder**
½ **teaspoon salt**
 2 **tablespoons shortening**
¾ **cup warm water**
  Vegetable oil for deep-frying
  Honey

1. Combine ¼ cup sugar and cinnamon in small bowl; set aside. Combine flour, remaining 2 teaspoons sugar, baking powder and salt in large bowl. Add shortening. With pastry blender or 2 knives, cut in shortening until mixture resembles fine crumbs. Gradually add water; stir with fork until mixture forms dough. Turn out onto lightly floured board; knead 2 minutes or until smooth. Shape into ball; cover with bowl and let rest 30 minutes.

2. Divide dough into 4 equal portions; shape each into ball. Flatten each ball to form circle about 8 inches in diameter and ⅛ inch thick. Cut each round into 4 wedges.

3. Pour oil into electric skillet or deep heavy skillet to depth of 1½ inches. Heat to 360°F. Cook dough, 2 pieces at a time, 2 minutes or until puffed and golden brown, turning once. Remove from oil with slotted spoon; drain on paper towels. Sprinkle with cinnamon-sugar mixture. Repeat with remaining sopaipillas. Serve warm with honey.

BAKED FLAN

Makes 10 (½-cup) servings

4 cups 2% milk
6 eggs
1 cup plus 2 tablespoons EQUAL® SPOONFUL*
2½ teaspoons vanilla
¼ teaspoon salt
    Sliced fresh fruit (optional)
    Fresh mint (optional)

*May substitute 27 packets EQUAL® sweetener.

• Heat milk just to simmering in medium saucepan. Let cool 5 minutes.

• Beat eggs, Equal®, vanilla and salt in large bowl until smooth. Gradually beat in hot milk. Pour mixture into 1½-quart casserole or ten 6-ounce custard cups.

• Place casserole or custard cups in roasting pan. Pour 1 inch of hot water into roasting pan. Bake in preheated 325°F oven 50 to 60 minutes or until knife inserted halfway between center and edge of custard comes out clean.

• Remove casserole or custard cups from roasting pan. Cool to room temperature on wire rack. Refrigerate several hours until well chilled.

• Serve garnished with sliced fresh fruit and mint, if desired.

MEXICAN COFFEE
WITH CHOCOLATE AND CINNAMON

Makes 10 to 12 servings

6 cups water
½ cup ground dark roast coffee
2 cinnamon sticks plus more for garnish
2 cups whipping cream, divided
⅓ cup chocolate syrup
¼ cup dark brown sugar, packed
1 teaspoon vanilla
¼ cup powdered sugar
½ teaspoon vanilla
Cinnamon

1. Place water in coffee maker. Add coffee and cinnamon sticks to the filter. Combine 1 cup whipping cream, chocolate syrup, brown sugar and vanilla in coffee pot. Brew coffee mixture so that coffee drips into coffee pot with chocolate cream mixture.

2. Meanwhile, whip remaining 1 cup whipping cream in large bowl. Sprinkle in powdered sugar and vanilla and beat until stiff peaks form. Pour coffee into individual coffee cups and top with whipped cream. Sprinkle with cinnamon.

Mexican Coffee with Chocolate and Cinnamon

The publisher would like to thank the companies and organizations listed below for the use of their recipes and photographs in this publication.

Birds Eye® Foods

Bob Evans®

Del Monte Corporation

Dole Food Company, Inc.

Equal® sweetener

The Golden Grain Company®

Guiltless Gourmet®

Lawry's® Foods

MASTERFOODS USA

Ortega®, A Division of B&G Foods, Inc.

Reckitt Benckiser Inc.

Sargento® Foods Inc.

StarKist Seafood Company

Unilever Foods North America

METRIC CONVERSION CHART

VOLUME MEASUREMENTS (dry)

$1/8$ teaspoon = 0.5 mL
$1/4$ teaspoon = 1 mL
$1/2$ teaspoon = 2 mL
$3/4$ teaspoon = 4 mL
1 teaspoon = 5 mL
1 tablespoon = 15 mL
2 tablespoons = 30 mL
$1/4$ cup = 60 mL
$1/3$ cup = 75 mL
$1/2$ cup = 125 mL
$2/3$ cup = 150 mL
$3/4$ cup = 175 mL
1 cup = 250 mL
2 cups = 1 pint = 500 mL
3 cups = 750 mL
4 cups = 1 quart = 1 L

VOLUME MEASUREMENTS (fluid)

1 fluid ounce (2 tablespoons) = 30 mL
4 fluid ounces ($1/2$ cup) = 125 mL
8 fluid ounces (1 cup) = 250 mL
12 fluid ounces ($1 1/2$ cups) = 375 mL
16 fluid ounces (2 cups) = 500 mL

WEIGHTS (mass)

$1/2$ ounce = 15 g
1 ounce = 30 g
3 ounces = 90 g
4 ounces = 120 g
8 ounces = 225 g
10 ounces = 285 g
12 ounces = 360 g
16 ounces = 1 pound = 450 g

DIMENSIONS

$1/16$ inch = 2 mm
$1/8$ inch = 3 mm
$1/4$ inch = 6 mm
$1/2$ inch = 1.5 cm
$3/4$ inch = 2 cm
1 inch = 2.5 cm

OVEN TEMPERATURES

250°F = 120°C
275°F = 140°C
300°F = 150°C
325°F = 160°C
350°F = 180°C
375°F = 190°C
400°F = 200°C
425°F = 220°C
450°F = 230°C

BAKING PAN SIZES

Utensil	Size in Inches/Quarts	Metric Volume	Size in Centimeters
Baking or Cake Pan (square or rectangular)	$8 \times 8 \times 2$	2 L	$20 \times 20 \times 5$
	$9 \times 9 \times 2$	2.5 L	$23 \times 23 \times 5$
	$12 \times 8 \times 2$	3 L	$30 \times 20 \times 5$
	$13 \times 9 \times 2$	3.5 L	$33 \times 23 \times 5$
Loaf Pan	$8 \times 4 \times 3$	1.5 L	$20 \times 10 \times 7$
	$9 \times 5 \times 3$	2 L	$23 \times 13 \times 7$
Round Layer Cake Pan	$8 \times 1 1/2$	1.2 L	20×4
	$9 \times 1 1/2$	1.5 L	23×4
Pie Plate	$8 \times 1 1/4$	750 mL	20×3
	$9 \times 1 1/4$	1 L	23×3
Baking Dish or Casserole	1 quart	1 L	—
	$1 1/2$ quart	1.5 L	—
	2 quart	2 L	—